HURDY GURDY DAYS

A portrait of Coventry at the
beginning of the Twentieth Century

THE WOMEN'S RESEARCH GROUP

i

The Women's Research Group was formed in 1998 after a series of lectures on women's history at Coventry University. A number of them were so concerned by the lack of information relating to local women, that they wanted to discover more about them. Just who were these women, commemorated only in the name of a road or a block of flats? Their first book *Redressing the Balance* published in 1999, consists of a number of profiles of women who have made a contribution to life in Coventry, in however small a way. *Hurdy Gurdy Days* deals with poverty in Coventry at the beginning of the twentieth century and how women dealt with its effects. The group continues to record and report on the lives of Coventry women.

Published by The Women's Group
First Edition 2001

Second Edition 2010

Cover photograph of
Beatrice & Florence Raby
c.1903

ISBN 978-0-9540604-0-4

Printed by C & J System Printers - Coventry

Introduction

Before Dr. Kenneth Richardson wrote his book *Twentieth Century Coventry* published in 1972, he collected oral evidence of the growth of the city as part of his research. The tapes were donated to Coventry University by his widow. *Hurdy Gurdy Days* by Beatrice Callow was amongst these tapes.

When I first heard the tape I was immediately impressed by its simplicity and honesty. I was incensed by the indignity that poverty brings, the insensitivity of the medical profession and how important the role of the woman was in the family. Throughout this account, the evidence shows that although men have the power, it is the women who have the strength. They are the ones that hold the family together, help their neighbours when they are in trouble and supplement family income when their husbands squander their meagre earnings in the public house. We also see what happens when the woman is weak or totally oppressed; the family falls into degradation and loses hope.

I knew I had to find out more about this period of Coventry's history and Beatrice Callow, the author of *Hurdy Gurdy Days*. First of all, however, I would like to present her story, slightly edited for easier reading, and attempt to address the many questions that arise afterwards. Instead of writing her memoir in the first person she used the device of writing as though she was the younger sister, whereas she was the elder of the two and the story is her own.

L. H.

Acknowledgements

I would like to thank Philip Callow for his permission to use the text of *Hurdy Gurdy Days*, as he owns the copyright of all his mother's writing. The part reproduced here is only a fraction of the whole work, which may be published in full at some time in the future. I am grateful too for the loan of family photographs reproduced in this book and for authorization to reproduce his poem *Mother.*

Many thanks to Arthur Owens of Coventry University Library for permission to use the recording of *Hurdy Gurdy Days*.

I am indebted to other members of the Callow family, especially David Callow and Dr. Callow who helped in my search for Beatrice Callow.

The staff of Coventry Records Office and the Local Studies Department of the Central Library for all their help.

Cathy Hunt for her proof reading and suggestions for improvements to my commentary.

Rev. Alan Munden, vicar of Christ Church, for directing me to Warwick Records Office for information about the activities of the pre-war church.

Hurdy Gurdy Days by Beatrice Callow

This is the story of Grace Charlton, a little girl who lived in Coventry in the early part of the twentieth century. It tells of the poverty and hardship endured by many of the working class people in those days.

1

Grace Charlton was born before the beginning of the century in Much Park Street. A street full of pubs and courts. She was the eldest child of one of the very poor families living in Coventry at that time.

The poor, squalid little houses we lived in looked as if they had grown there, but hundreds of years ago there was a park around there, hence the name of our street. There was also Little Park Street and Parkside. In Little Park Street there were courts like ours and some very old buildings. There was a very large house standing back behind some iron railings, and we often wondered who lived there.

The town was full of hovels like ours owned by people with money to invest, not caring about anything except making money. We paid 3/6d per week and our grandparents had lived there all their lives, having been born there. Nothing had ever been done in the nature of repairs as far back as they could remember, so it was a good investment - 14 houses at 3/6d per week.

There was only one door to each of the houses in the court. No back door and two small windows at the front, one upstairs and one downstairs. The door of the next house almost touched, and this was repeated all the way up the yard. There was no privacy even inside the houses as the neighbours could hear the arguments and rows, and there were plenty of these, and fights, caused by the drink.

Inside the front door was a room about 12ft by 10ft, where absolutely everything had to be done. Halfway up the wall was a sort of matchboard panelling, painted dark brown and above that was a faded wallpaper, where it had'nt peeled off through the damp.

The washing-up had to be done on the deal top table in an enamel bowl with a tin tray to drain the crocks, as there was no sink or draining board. There was an old-fashioned fireplace with hobs on each side and an oven on one side, which took up the whole of one wall of the room. All the cooking and hot water for washing clothes had to be done on this fire, the water for washing clothes being heated in a huge iron pot on a sort of grid across the fire. There was always a roaring fire, and in summer the heat was unbearable.

There were four lavatories, or closets as they were called, to the 14 houses in the court. These were right at the top of the yard in what was called the back yard. They were earth closets and were emptied by the 'night men'. A row of dustbins, one to each house had to be emptied too. The slops went down the one and only drain by the water tap in the middle of the yard, which served everybody.

When it was fine all the children who lived in the court used to play in the back yard amongst the dustbins and closets and under the lines of washing. There was always somebody's washing hanging out, as the women had nowhere else to hang it and had to take turns for the lines. A mangle with huge rollers and a big wheel to turn them stood by the tap. It had stood there so long that nobody seemed to know to whom it belonged. Our gran said it belonged to her, but everybody used it in turn. It had to be screwed down tightly by means of a turn-screw at the top. This brought the rollers together, but it had stood outside in all weathers so long it used to creak and groan. The rollers had a great gap between them through years of wear and tear. When it rained or snowed the women used to have to go out and mangle with a sack round their shoulders and one over their heads, sometimes they wore their husband's cloth cap with the poke at the back. That is if he didn't happen to be wearing it.

The hot water from the huge iron pot on the fire was emptied into a dolly tub, usually a wooden one with metal hoops around it, obtained from the brewery over the wall. The dolly had three short handles attached to the top of the spindle and at the bottom was a wooden contraption with a metal strip round it. It was our gran's dolly really and it was very old-fashioned. The clothes were put into the tub and bumped up and down by the dolly, then lifted up by a stick to be put through the mangle rollers.

There was a draining-board in front of the rollers with an opening for the water to go through and at the back of the mangle an old zinc bath would be placed with clean water in it for rinsing. The clothes went through the rollers with the dirty water dropping back into the dolly tub at the front. Then they had to be mangled backwards from the clean water in the zinc bath, taking care not to let them fall into the tub again. The draining board could be tilted at an angle to prevent this from happening. They were then transferred to a wicker clothes basket and taken up to the back yard to dry, if possible, with children playing underneath them and neighbours going backwards and forwards to the dustbins and closets.

If it was a wet day the clothes were festooned across the living room on lines, sheets and everything else, to dry by the fire, the water dripping on to the table and floor. There always seemed to be washing about. When it was dry it had to be ironed by means of a flat iron fixed to a sort of grid in front of the fire, which hooked on to the bars. It used to get very hot, and I have seen our mam spit on it to test the heat. The spit would sizzle and run off. Two irons were used, one after the other. An old piece of blanket was put on top of the table to iron on and a two-way heavy metal ring for an iron stand. We used to make iron holders for mam for Christmas presents. Sometimes the clothes would stay on the lines in the living room until Thursday or Friday. Then the whole business of washing would start again on Monday. No wonder people caught colds and died of T.B.

Our Grace used to run errands for everybody in the court, taking babies out in old broken-down perambulators, for which she sometimes, only sometimes, received a halfpenny. The perambulators were a sort of wicker armchair affair, with two long handles coming out from underneath somewhere and two metal props to act as a sort of brake. There was no hood on the ones the neighbours in our court could afford. How the poor babies ever kept dry when it rained, I don't know. Grace used to push these contraptions about with two babies in sometimes, one at each end, as well as the groceries. She used to push these down the sides and at the back of the pillow. There were always plenty of babies to take out. They were more plentiful than money. There was always more shopping to do on Saturday mornings. The money was all gone by Monday or Tuesday, when a visit to 'Uncle' would be necessary.

In addition to running errands and baby minding, Grace had to help mam do the cleaning on Saturday morning, as she was the eldest and considered old enough. The tiny living room would look like a cafe when it was closed, as all the chairs would be put on the table off the floor, so that the dirt could be swept into the fireplace. The fender also had to go on the table on some newspaper. It had a steel top, which had to be rubbed with emery paper, until it shone like a mirror. The grate was black-leaded and that had to be cleaned too. The black-lead was in a tin to which had been added a little water, then a dubby sort of brush was pressed on to the sticky mess and squashed round and round, then put on to the hobs and front of the grate. 'Don't forget the bars' our mam would shout. So of course all this had to be done before the fire could be lit, and in the winter it was perishing cold as this was our only heat in the house

The long fire irons, which were kept in the fender, had to be rubbed with emery paper too and put on the table with the fender. Then the hearth had to be whitened with a hearthstone and left to dry. It looked lovely while it was clean, but had to be done regularly to keep it nice and clean.

Meanwhile all the knives, forks and spoons had to be cleaned, the knives rubbed on a knife-board on which bath-brick had been sprinkled.

We both hated all this cleaning on Saturday mornings. It was so cold and uncomfortable especially in the depth of winter. Grace didn't mind the scrubbing of the deal top table and the red tiled floor so much. At least you could see something for all your trouble, but all that knife cleaning and black-leading was, to her way of thinking, a waste of time. No sooner was it all done and looking spick and span when, for instance, the black-leaded kettle which always stood on the hob, would boil and spit all over the nice whitened hearth.

In the middle of all these chores the rent man would call. He would tap tap tap on the door with his walking stick, startling us all. mam used to say it might be the police coming to arrest our Dad for being drunk and disorderly, which she often dreaded as he was so argumentative and quarrelsome when he was drunk. She used to warn him about it, but he only sneered and snarled back at her. 'Gerr----off wi' yer, yom ollers worritin over somat.'

We would stand still and look at one another for a second or so every time and mam would peer through the window, pulling the lace curtain to one side. 'Oh, it's only Mr Dexter,' she would say with a sigh of relief, 'Open the door.' Mr Dexter was a tall, gaunt man about 6ft. tall, very upright, as if he had a rod up his back. He had a sanctimonious voice, a long thin face and wore pince-nez type spectacles on his nose.

He would say, 'Good morning, rent please.' His time never varied or his voice. We needn't have worried about who it was, but we always did. mam would say, 'Just a minute Mr Dexter,' and reach up to the mantle-shelf over the fireplace where she always kept the rent book, together with the 3/6d, all ready for him. If she asked him to do any repairs, the answer was always the same, 'No repairs madam,' but he always pocketed the rent.

2

Mrs Graves lived next door but one to us and had twin boys. She was a poor, frail little woman, with a drunken husband who used to take most of his wages to the pub, leaving only a small amount on which to run the house and provide food for him and the children. She always seemed to be having babies, which rarely lived past birth. The twins were just about alive and that was all. They were poor specimens of humanity.

Mrs Graves used to live in dread and fear of her husband. He used to come staggering up the yard after being in the pub for two or three hours, drunk as a lord. Before he had been in the house five minutes a piercing scream would be heard, the door would open and he would throw her out, her head banging against the brick wall opposite. She would drag herself up somehow and stumble back to protect her babies, only to come out again in a few minutes. This went on for about half an hour, until his drunken rage had spent itself and he had fallen asleep over his supper, which was the reason for his temper, it not being ready on the table when he chose to come in.

That poor woman must have been black and blue with bruises as this was a frequent occurrence, but none of the neighbours interfered. They were all scared of him and kept out of his way and he enjoyed being a tyrant. The twins eventually died. Then the woman herself died, having no strength left to put up with his brutality. No authorities intervened. There was no welfare state in those days. That poor, unhappy woman had to go to the workhouse, because she was too exhausted to carry on. If our Grace had been older I am sure she would have seen that he was brought to justice for his cruelty. As it was, I can remember how she used to rock those two babies in the cradle. They were so weak they could only whine and whimper.

4

Our mam used to warn her about going into that house, but she still went. As soon as Mrs Graves heard her husband's hob-nailed boots on the cobbled yard, she would say to Grace, 'Goo'arn quick 'e's coming,' and Grace would dash out of the house as fast as her little legs would carry her, through the one and only door and up the yard to our house, never stopping until she was safe inside with the door bolted.

He would see her run out of his door and curse and swear, shaking his fist at her, shouting, 'Yer bloody little swine. Leave my kids alone. I'll wallop y're arse for yet when I git 'old on yer,' but he never got the chance. Grace's heart would be pounding away underneath her frock and our mam would say, 'One o' these days he'll catch yer me gel.'

After his wife died Mr Graves lived alone. He took to drinking heavily and owing to lack of proper nourishment, he became ill and couldn't work, so he got the sack from his job. He died a terrible death with cancer of the stomach. His cries could be heard all over the court. Eventually he had to be taken to the workhouse infirmary, as the neighbours refused to do anything for him and after about a month he died.

In the next court our Grace had a little friend called Nellie Brookes, and sometimes she used to go round and play with her. Nellie was the eldest of eleven children. Their house was even worse than ours; their mother seemed to have lost interest completely. The house and children were dirty and she always seemed to be bending over the hot fire, either cooking or washing. She cooked enormous quantities of spuds in their jackets, in a huge iron saucepan, which she used to lift on to the table. The spuds were ladled out two or three at a time, on to the eleven enamel plates, which never seemed to have been washed. They were nearly raw, as there never seemed to be time to wait for them to cook properly, as the children were always hungry. Spuds seemed to be their only food, as they couldn't afford meat or fish. They never sat down; there simply wasn't room, so they all stood around the table making a terrible din.

The door always seemed to be open, even in winter, as the children used to run in and out at all hours of the day, other people's children as well and the floor was as dirty as the road outside. Grace would go in and stand by Nellie at the table, sticking a fork into a spud in the iron saucepan standing in the middle of the table.

Mrs Brookes was a frail looking woman always coughing, doubled up from the everlasting bending over the fire and the dolly tub, which stood over in one corner. The water in the tub was filthy dirty and seemed to be used over and over again, because Mrs Brookes hadn't got the strength to keep carrying the water from the tap outside in the yard. There was always washing festooned across the room like ours, on lines of string, dripping all over the floor even worse than ours, as they had no mangle like us, such as it was and Mrs Brookes couldn't ring very tightly.

She must have been very pretty, our mam used to say, before they had all those

5

children and before her husband took nearly all his wages to the pub, and beat her if his dinner wasn't ready when he came home. Her hair was a lovely chestnut brown colour then and she had lovely brown eyes. Nellie had inherited her mother's colouring. Nellie's clothes were always in rags and she hardly ever had boots on, even in winter. What she had got her mother used to have to cadge. She always had a running nose, 'candles' the other kids called it. Her neck was covered in tiny red spots caused by fleas and bugs and she was continually scratching her body and head. All the other children were like that too in that house. Always scratching like monkeys.

Although Grace was only just turned five, she was puzzled as to where all those children kept coming from, because they were so poor, but of course she was too young to understand. One day when mam was combing her hair ready for school, she saw something moving. 'Hold still will yet,' cried mam and kept parting her hair looking and looking. 'Oh, I'll be late, let me go. I'll git the cane,' cried Grace. 'Oh, all right goo on then, but don't git playing wi' that Nellie Brookes. She's dirty and yor catching dicks off her. What's the use tryin' ter keep yor 'air clane if her will play wi'er. That's wheere we're getting all the fleas from as well, from theere 'ouse.'

'Well she can't 'elp it, mam,' said Grace.

'Well, if I catch yer goin' in theere agin I'll gie yor backside a tannin' that I will,' said mam.

Grace still played with Nellie as she didn't like to tell her what mam had said, but only outside in the yard. Until one day Nellie's mother called her to come and have her dinner.

'Yo can come in wi' me,' said Nellie to Grace, but when they got to the door Grace remembered what mam had said about a tannin' if she went in that house again, so she stood outside on the doorstep.

'Come in can't yer,' shouted Nellie's mother. 'What yer standing theere for? What's the matter wi' yer all of a sudden. Come on,' she went on, 'Yo've bin in ere afore.'

But Grace stood still on the step, hanging her head and muttering something about 'I can't.'

'Why can't yer?' yelled Mrs Brookes and Grace started to cry.

'Oh come on in and stop blubberin',' said Mrs Brookes.

'I cccaan't I tell yer,' sobbed Grace. 'Me mam says I'll have a tannin' on me backside if I come inside yor 'ouse again, cos yor 'ouse is dirty and yo've got a lot of fleas and bugs, as well as dicks wot move in yer 'air, an' I'm catchin' 'em off of yer.'

Mrs Brookes stood staring at Grace, flabbergasted, trembling from head to foot. At last she found her voice and said, 'What's that yer say. Our ouse is dirty. Oh yer mam said that, did she? Wheere's me 'at an' coat? Dinner or no dinner, I'll gie her a piece of me mind I know.'

6

Poor Grace was still crying and was now frightened out of her wits. She didn't know you should never say things like that to people's faces, only behind their backs. Mrs Brookes rushed out of the house, down the yard and round to our court. She banged on the door and mam went all unsuspecting to answer. As soon as she opened it, Mrs Brookes all agitated and excited, wringing her hands, started yelling and swearing.

'What the bloody 'ell do yer mean by saying my kids and our 'ouse is dirty, yer cheeky bitch? Who do yer think yo are? Let me tell yer we'r as clane as what yo are and I'll see our Nellie don't play with yor kids agin, don't yo bother, or 'as any mower spuds at our table along wi' our kids.' All the time taking her coat off and rolling up her sleeves.

'Whatever are yer talking about?' says our mam, all red and shaking, as by now there was a crowd behind Mrs Brookes. All listening and waiting for a fight.

'Our Grace told yer I said that? You wait till I git 'old on her, I'll wallop 'er backside for her, I know. Wheere is she?' Looking up and down the yard. 'Telling fibs like that.'

Mrs Brookes just didn't know what to say now and thought perhaps the kid was making it up, and after a minute or two she started rolling her sleeves down, but swearing as she went away and shouting, 'She must 'ave gorrit from somewheere. Don't yer worry I'll find out,' shaking her fist at mam.

Mam shut the door quick and stood for a minute with her back to it after locking it, saying to herself. 'Good lor', that was a near thing. Yo wait till our Grace comes 'ome, I'll tan 'er backside for 'er repeating what I say. She's old enough to know better.'

Poor Grace was only over the wall and heard all this rowing and shouting. She was crying to herself and ran behind the brewery drays to hide until it was dark, but she was very frightened, cold and hungry. After a while she thought she had better go home and face our mam, who must have calmed down by now. So she crept up the yard and listened outside the door, but there was no sound coming from inside and no light either. Mam must have gone to look for her, she thought. She opened the door very quietly and slowly went in. Then she screamed, as she was pulled further into the room, with blows on her head and shoulders. Mam had been waiting behind the door knowing Grace would come home when it got dark, as she was afraid of that. She was in such a temper that she shook poor Grace, thumped her and ran her up the stairs to bed, hitting her legs and backside with a cane as she went. Grace couldn't speak and was sobbing bitterly.

When I went to bed she was still crying, and I said, 'Never mind Grace, don't cry,' but all she could say between her sobs was, 'We--ll mam did s-ay they were dirty, she did s-ay it, she d-id. Why d-id she te-ll Mrs Brookes she didn't? She w-as telling fibs not me. Why d-id she h-it me l-ike that?' Poor Grace. It is hard to understand the grown-up world of hypocracy when you are a child.

7

3

The brewery yard, which was just over the wall from the courts, was a great attraction to all the children in the street, including Grace. At the entrance was the house where the manager lived with his family. It was a very old-fashioned house, but to Grace it was a palace compared with ours, for one thing it had a front and side door.

The side door was in a covered entry where the horses and drays used to go to be loaded up with barrels of beer. Through the entry it led out to a wide, open yard where the horses were stabled and covered wagons were kept. The children who lived in the brewery house were better clothed and better behaved than most of the children of the courts. Their mother was a tailoress and she made waistcoats for gentry, working for a local tailor in the town. Sometimes she had piles and piles of work to do and would sit for hours working far into the night, when the children were in bed, at her sewing machine, treadling away with her feet and guiding the garment through with her hands.

Their name was Gibberd and there were two boys and two girls. The oldest boy, about a year older than Grace, was called Tom, then came Amy, then Jackie who was four and Nancy who was two. Tom being the oldest, had a sort of fatherly attitude towards all the other children, and as Grace was such a little thing for her age, she seemed to create a protective urge in him and she in turn always looked up to him. Some of the other boys were rough and she hated them. They were cruel, nasty things, she thought. Particularly one big boy who used to follow her about and try to get her to go to the 'back-yard' when he knew none of the other children would be there. She was scared of him, but she daren't tell mam. He reckoned without Tom though, who threatened what he would do to him if he didn't leave her alone.

Their favourite game was mothers and fathers. Tom was always the father, and because of that, Grace always wanted to be the mother. But Tom said she wasn't big enough, so a girl named Evelyn Ward from a court across the street was chosen. Grace had to be content to be one of their children. Real mothers and fathers in our street had lots of children, so there was always a big crowd of us in the covered wagon, which we pretended was our house.

Despite all the poverty and drunkenness all around us, the games we used to play in those covered wagons were some of the happiest. As the children all grew up they lost touch with one another, but we never lost sight of Evelyn Ward from the court across the street. Our Evelyn, as her mother always called her and Amy Gibberd from the brewery house, grew up with us as we all went to the same Sunday School, even after we left the court and moved to another district further away. Just inside the court across the street where Evelyn Ward lived was a little stone house, very quaint and very old and from what I can remember there was a family living in it. We often played with the children in that court, it was nicer than ours somehow.

On either side of the court were two shops, on the right was a greengrocers shop and on the left was a haberdashery shop, where they sold everything you could imagine. Grace was always looking in the window of this shop. It seemed to have a special attraction for her, as there was a lot of cheap jewellery set out on glass shelves, which seemed to sparkle, especially in the lamplight. An elderly brother and sister kept the shop, which had been handed down by their parents.

Grace used to be rather scared of 'old Dukes'. He was a tall thin man with a stiff, winged white collar, a long shabby coat and he wore pince-nez glasses attached to a long chain. When anybody entered the shop a bell on the door would ring, ting-a-ling, and he would appear from behind a curtain at the back somewhere, look over the top of his glasses and say 'Yes?' in such an austere voice that if Grace went into the shop with anybody else, she would hide behind them. His sister, Miss Dukes, was also tall and thin, with her grey hair combed upwards into a knot on top of her head. She had a long neck and wore a high-collared blouse, reaching almost to her ears. She also wore eye-glasses the same type as her brother, with a chain attached to a safety pin on her blouse. Grace was not so scared of Miss Dukes and when she wanted to buy anything she would watch the window to find out what time each of them went for their meal. If Miss Dukes kept coming into the shop every time the bell rang she would know Mr Dukes was having a meal.

In the window there were some rings like blue enamel butterfly wings. So pretty, Grace thought. How she would love one of them. She looked in that window for weeks while she saved her halfpennies earned from taking the washing backwards and forwards to the gentry for our mam and the neighbours. Sometimes her tiny arms ached from stretching them around the wide baskets of washing. Now she had saved three halfpennies, but as the tray of rings was not marked with a price ticket, she didn't know how much they were. There were other rings on the tray, plain gold rings, which looked very nice, but she liked the blue enamel butterfly rings the best. At last one day when 'old Dukes' had gone to have his tea, she darted boldly into the shop, clutching her precious three halfpennies.

'How much are the blue enamel butterfly rings in the window please?' she asked Miss Dukes in a timid voice, barely reaching the counter.

Over to the window went Miss Dukes removing all sorts of articles to get to the tray of rings at the front, which she brought to the counter for Grace to look at. She stood on tiptoes to see them better. How lovely they all looked she thought, the blue enamel rings shining in the light of the lamp hanging over the counter. The plain gold rings looked lovely too, but she really liked the blue enamel rings the best. Miss Dukes said,

'The blue enamel rings are sixpence each and the plain gold rings are one-and-a-half pence.'

9

Poor Grace's heart sank and her dream of possessing one of the pretty enamel rings faded as she had only got three halfpennies clutched tightly in her hand. This was three-week's washing earnings and sixpence would take such a long time to save and all the rings might be gone by then. There was a silence while she gazed at all the glittering rings on the tray and wondered what to do. It was broken by Miss Dukes saying,

'Come along. Do make up your mind child. I can't stand here all night.'

Grace looked up at her with a pleading look in her eyes, but Miss Dukes said,

'Let me see how much money you have got.' Grace opened her hand. 'Oh! You have only got one-and-a-half pence,' sounding so like her brother now, only with a higher pitched voice. 'Well then you had better have a plain gold ring. Just try one on for size.' Grace tried one after the other on her tiny finger. At last Miss Dukes began to lose patience and suggested she could tie some cotton round and round her finger above the ring to stop it slipping over her knuckle, so Grace gave Miss Dukes her three halfpennies and came out of the shop feeling like a queen now that she had a gold ring on her finger and kept stopping to admire it by of the shop window.

When she got home, our mam caught her taking it on and off her finger and holding out her hand to the lighted lamp on the table to make it sparkle.

'Whatever 'ave yer got theere,' shouted mam, pulling Grace towards her, but she put her hand behind her back and hung her head. Mam said,

'Come on, lets have a look,' and Grace slowly put out her hand showing the ring.

'Well, well, if it ain't a wedding ring. Wheere on earth 'ave yet got that thing from?'

Grace said in a trembling voice, on the verge of tears, 'From Dukes, and it ain't a thing. It's a gold ring. I bought it with me own money. It was one-and-a-half pence. I saved up for three wicks.'

'Well yo can tek it back,' yelled Mam, 'Tek it back I say at once.' Grace backed away into the corner of the room hiding her hand and starting to cry. Take her precious gold ring back after all that saving. Oh, whatever should she do.

Mam rushed across to the door and snatching the coat off the peg, pulled Grace along with her saying, 'It's no good blartin', come on.' When they got over to the shop, mam marched straight in and 'old Dukes' came from behind the curtain, it being his turn to serve.

'Yes?' he said in that austere voice of his. For once Grace was thankful Mam was there.

'I'll gie yer Yes,' shouted mam at the top of her voice, 'Selling a brass wedding ring to a little 'un of five for one-and-a-half pence. I'll have the law on yer I will.'

'Old Dukes' looked a bit agitated and said, 'I didnt serve her,' and called his sister into the shop. She seemed as scared of him as Grace was. 'Did you serve this child with this ring?' he said to his sister.

'Yes, she chose that one,' said Miss Dukes.

'Well, 'ere is yer ring back. Now gie 'er 'er money back,' said mam throwing it on the counter and after a bit more arguing 'old Dukes' went to a drawer and took out a penny and a half penny and gave it to mam and out of the shop they went. 'I'll gie yer waste yer money on that trash,' said Mam to Grace, who was sobbing her heart out. All her dreams shattered after looking in the window all those weeks and saving up her half pennies. She didn't know it was a wedding ring as mam called it. She never went into that shop again. It was a crime to mam to waste one-and-a-half pence on that rubbish as we were so poor, it was a struggle enough to live at all. We could only afford the cheapest pieces of meat and bacon bits.

At the grocers just round the corner in Earl Street, bits of bacon were put on the counter, which were left over from the slicer. Often these bits were very fat and the rind very thick, but Grace used to ask for three pennyworth of bacon bits and had to have whatever the assistant gave her.

4

Grace attended the school she had started at when she was three years old. She hated it and mam was always afraid she would run away. She was a quiet child and just used to sit on the form in the classroom and never utter a sound unless spoken to by a teacher, who scared her. The school was St. Michael's and was the church school for St. Michael's church and was used for day and Sunday school. Our dad and mam were married in St. Michael's church when they were twenty years of age and both Grace and I were christened there. It later became the Coventry Cathedral.

The school was built of stone with windows high up in the wall, making it impossible to see out of them from the classroom. There was a heavy oak door, which only the teachers were able to open. It was very old and used to creak and groan on its hinges. Into this door trooped all the children, boys and girls, from the playground, which was surrounded by a high stone wall with a big iron gate in the middle, which the teacher used to clang to, when the last child was in - and woe betide the late comers.

Precisely at 9am a big bell rang and all the children would get into line upon orders from the teachers. As they all filed into the school through the lobby, where all the hats and coats were hung, one of the favourite boys would be told to watch the gate and wait there until after prayers, which were read and led by the headmistress who lived in the schoolhouse next door to the school. She wore a black crinoline dress and gave the impression of floating into the room, as her feet were hidden under the dress. Her hair was dressed in long sausage curls caught together in a bunch at the back of her head by means of a comb and she looked just like the pictures of Queen Victoria.

When prayers were over, one of the teachers would go to the door and call the boy detailed to watch the gate, who would come into the classroom and report how many children were outside. These poor, unfortunate children were then let in by the teacher and sent to the headmistress, whom everybody feared, to be caned regardless of the reason why they were late. No excuse whatever was accepted, consequently every morning at our house between eight and nine, it was a war of nerves.

'Urry up. Urry up.'

'Oh! What's the time, I'll be late.'

'Don't wan' any mower breakfast.'

'Well, tek some lunch then.' Mam used to say, wrapping the thick slices of bread and lard or dripping (never butter) in newspaper and running out of the door into the street looking to the right, then the left to see if there were other children about.

'Oh! Yes, there's Nellie Brookes, she's never late.' Breathing a sigh of relief.

One afternoon, soon after Grace had started school, she was only three remember, and during a sewing lesson where all the girls had to learn to sew (goodness knows what the boys did) a Miss Sutcliff handed every child a needle and a piece of white cotton. Whether she made a mistake, or had such a large class and was so busy she didn't notice, the needle which she gave to Grace had such a tiny hole even a grown-up person would not have been able to thread it. Anyway, our Grace couldn't thread that needle. The white cotton became black and all screwed up. In the end, when one of the other children had to leave the room, Grace young as she was, saw her opportunity and fled through the open door, out through the big iron gates, which mercifully for Grace were open to allow the coalman through and down the street as fast as her little legs could carry her, crying all the way, 'I can't fred the needle. I can't fred the needle.'

By the time she reached home all the neighbours knew why she had run away from school and why she was crying, going on to one another about mam sending her at all at that age.

Mrs Trapp who lived at the first house in the court was very fond of Grace and carried on alarming, saying to Mam. 'If yo don't tek 'er back and pull that theer teacher's 'air owt, I will. The bitch, pickin' on a little un like 'er.' And she would have done too. There was no mincing matters with Mrs Trapp.

By morning Grace had quietened down, so mam went to school with her, watched by all the neighbours, to give the teacher a piece of her mind. Miss Sutcliff was one of two sisters. The old one was much more austere than the younger one, who was only about eighteen years of age, with hair worn in a pigtail down her back, the fashion of the day. Mam couldn't get out of Grace which of these sisters had given her the needle to thread, so she yelled at both of them at the top of her voice.

12

'I'll pull that theere pig-tail off yor 'ead if yo do that again.' She threatened the younger sister. On hearing that remark the older sister came forward and apologised to mam and said it was her, but she was very sorry and had been busy with the other children and hadn't noticed that the needle she had given Grace had such a tiny hole. She promised it wouldn't happen again, but it was hard work to get Grace to go to school after that scene.

Just up the road from the school was the 14th century Whitefriars Monastery, now being used as a Workhouse. All the children of school age had to attend St. Michael's school as it was the nearest. They all sat together, boys and girls, on forms at one side of the classroom away from the other children. They were poorly clad in sack-like navy blue dresses for the girls and rough serge trousers for the boys. The girls had scanty underclothing. When they wanted 'to leave the room' they were invariably afraid to ask and often 'did everything' all over the form and on to the floor. They were always being punished for their dirty habits.

These poor half-starved, ill-mannered children, who nobody cared about or wanted, had to come to school by law. Grace somehow always managed to sit at the end of a row near to them. She knew they were different, but although she was sorry for them in her way, they were very rude to her, pulling faces and putting out their tongues at her. The workhouse children all had their heads shaved, because it was easier to keep them clean and as mam found it difficult to keep Grace's hair clean, she took her down to the barber's shop one Saturday morning and he shaved off all her hair too. Mam told Grace to keep away from the workhouse children, because of their dirty habits and bad manners, but now her hair had been shaved off like theirs she thought it didn't matter, so she still sat at the end of the row as near to them as she could.

Every day when she went back to school after dinner, Mam used to give her a farthing to spend at the sweet shop on the way. The sweets she bought were 4oz for 1d, so Grace got about six sweets for a farthing - 1oz. She was always fascinated by Mrs Berry at the sweet shop serving her, as she made up her own bags by screwing up a piece of newspaper into a cornet shape after weighing the sweets on scales with a brass scoop, polished bright, balanced on three brass chains coming down from a hook, with the same on the other side where the brass weights were, also polished bright. The sweets were displayed in the window in little glass dishes with white paper doylies in each dish, no bottles, they were on shelves inside the shop with boiled sweets in, at 2oz for 1d.

There was another sweet shop at the other end of the street between two pubs, where they sold home-made toffee in a square tin on the counter, with a shiny little hammer alongside to break it up into small pieces before putting it on the scales. They also sold homemade rock in sticks and cut it up with pincers.

5

Our gran, dad's mam, lived with us. At least we lived with her, as it was her house, such as it was. She had lived there all her life, as had her parents before her. Our grandfather had died long before we were born. Apparently gran had given birth to more children, but they had all died with convulsions, which was very prevalent in those days because of bad feeding. One of them, a girl, had lived to be about ten years old, but had died with a brain haemorrhage.

Our dad had suffered a very hard childhood. His mother had to go out to work doing other people's washing for a few bob, leaving him as soon as he could walk, to run about the yard with a tin bottle tied round his neck with milk and water in it. The neighbours used to keep an eye on him, but they had their own problems and if he didn't cry and yell, they didn't bother about anything else. Consequently, when his mother came home worn out and tired after a day at the wash-tub, he would run down the yard to meet her with his pants full and bow-legged, stinking to high heaven, expecting her to pick him up. Instead she would box his ears, which made him yell and send him staggering away from her. Poor gran, no wonder when she got old she snapped and snarled at everybody, sneering at us being brought up like 'fine ladies' as she called it.

'Ain't natchrel, living 'ere. They'll turn out bad uns, yo mark me words.'

She sent dad to school at three years of age, the same as Grace was when she went. He went to the same school, St. Michael's and left on the 17th April 1888 at the age of eleven. The schoolmaster gave him a certificate, which was called a labour certificate, which had to be handed to his first employer. This was the grocers round the corner in Earl Street. The same shop where later Grace bought the three pennyworth of bacon bits. He started as an errand boy for 2/6d per week.

Gran was a small woman with straight raven-black hair, which she wore in a Madonna style with a bob in the nape of the neck, with a very wide parting in the middle of her head. She had large brown eyes, which seemed to look right through you. In high society she would have been considered a beauty, but her life had been so terribly hard it had coarsened her and she had been more concerned with the struggle for existence for herself and our dad than to bother about her appearance. Although she was sixty years of age, her hair was still jet-black, but she was very deaf and always imagined everybody was talking about her and poking fun at her. She only had one tooth left at the front, the others having fallen out over the years and this one tooth looked like a big fang. When she got in a temper over anything, she would hiss and snarl like an old witch, the fang being loose, would move about in her mouth and we were terrified at being left alone with her.

In some strange way she loved Grace, but she didn't care for me, because I resembled mam and Grace was like our dad. We never saw her dressed up, she always used to wear her coarse 'epron' and a man's cap on her head, with the peak to the back and wore hob-nailed boots on her feet. Her longest journey was to the

Dullerton ave.

£ 160.000

connells

open house 23 apr.

rWinsford ave

£ 200.00

LPC

Chetwode close

£180.000 | allsop

Dulverton ave.

£180.000 - over

eh estates

Harewood rd

£474,950

Payne orro

pub at the bottom of the yard to have a jug filled every night with a pint of ale for a few coppers. She would then put it on the hob, make up a roaring fire and to the accompaniment of the crickets in the hearth, it would sizzle and bubble. Then she put the poker in the fire and when it was red hot she would plunge it into the beer in a jug with a loud hiss and that was her supper, with a noggin' of bread, cheese and onion.

Grace and I used to wait for her to start on her supper, because then she would pull up her skirt as high as ever she could, so that the hot fire would warm right up her legs. She wore what she called 'open drawers' and the heat of the fire would make her smell horrible. She was a very crude old woman, deaf as a post and didn't care for anybody. When she wanted to pass water at night time, she would go into a sort of cubby-hole under the stairs where a bucket was kept for all of us to use in case of emergency, to save going right up the back-yard in the dark. She would squat on top of the bucket, making a loud noise, which sounded as though the lock gates of the canal had opened. She couldn't hear it herself being so deaf. She wouldn't care anyway. Grace and I used to hide our faces with shame. If she saw us and our mam wasn't there, she would hiss and snarl at us, frightening us to death.

The neighbours all knew her and if mam had to go out anywhere, which she did sometimes to earn a shilling or two waiting at tables or washing up, she would ask them to listen and if they heard any screaming or crying to come in. But they never did as they were as scared of her as we were. Mam knew we were frightened of being left alone with gran, but she had no choice. We were so in need of the money she earned as dad spent every evening at the pub at the bottom of the yard.

At the first house in the court there lived a family named Trapp. There were two sons, as far as I can remember and two daughters. One of them was just like her mother, jolly and always laughing and the other one was very quiet and shy. Perhaps she took after the father whom we never saw, as he was away in the army. It was easy to get recruits for the regular army in those days, as there was so much unemployment. The men were sent abroad and were away from home for long periods. Their wives used to go and meet them when they did come home to make sure of getting a fair share of their pay, before it was spent at the pubs on the way home.

Mrs Trapp was a large, fat woman, always washing and working for other people as well as for her own family. Mam used to say she had a heart of gold. When there was any sickness around and anybody wanted help, it was always, 'Send for Mrs Trapp, she'll come.' She used to deliver the babies and 'lay out' after death.

There always seemed to be plenty of coming and going then. The undertakers and publicans must have done a roaring trade. To provide the money for a decent burial a penny a week was paid into a club. Everybody wore deep mourning at funerals. Most families had a new baby every year, with a midwife in attendance, usually a middle-aged woman past child bearing herself.

Grace was a great favourite with the Trapp family. In the afternoon when she came home from school, she would go into their house and have a cup of tea. Mrs Trapp had no teeth (nobody had dentures in those days), so she had to soften her pieces of bread in the tea and get them out with a spoon. She told Grace they were little fishes. Grace used to enjoy watching her get them out. She loved Mrs Trapp.

Our gran had one sister, whose name was Martha. So very different was Martha from our gran. There had been nine in the family and gran and Martha were the only survivors, the rest having died either at birth or in childhood. Martha's children were all grown up when her husband, Uncle Will, died and left her a widow.

She had been quite comfortably off during her married life. They had a nice little house with a very long garden, in a quiet street in a select neighourhood, far above our house in Much Park Street. She never came to see us and gran used to say she was 'stuck up'. Mam liked her and sometimes on a Sunday afternoon in the summer, she would take us to visit her, as it was on the outskirts of the town and more or less in the country. We used to love to go, as Uncle Will had lots of fruit bushes at the bottom of the garden and we made excuses to go down there.

Martha was very house-proud. When we descended on her unexpectedly, she would rush and lock the parlour door as she saw us coming in the gate. In the parlour there was a suite of green plush furniture, consisting of a sofa, two armchairs and four small chairs, all to match. The cushions on the sofa were never out of place. There was linoleum on the floor, with a black sealskin rug in front of the fireplace, a brass fender and fire irons, all polished bright and an aspidistra in a green pot on a stand in the centre of the window. The lace curtains were looped back with green silk cord. The room was only used on very special occasions like Christmas and birthdays. There was no piano; they hadn't been able to afford that. Our mam did envy this grandeur and was miserable for days after we had been on a visit, saying every time that she wouldn't go there again, but she did.

Martha had four children of her own, two boys and two girls, who were very well behaved. Uncle Will was a shoemaker by trade and we were always fascinated by him. He had a very deep voice and an enormous stomach. He used to sit in the corner by the fire in a big armchair, smoking a long-stemmed clay pipe, which seemed to rest on his large stomach.

After he died Martha had to give up her nice little home and go and live with her daughter Annie. Poor, inoffensive Martha, how she must have grieved. Annie's husband was consumptive and she had to take in washing to keep their three children. She had a very hard life and there couldn't have been much comfort for poor Martha. Annie's husband's name was Ben. He was a very quiet sort of chap, very tall and extremely thin. He had a terrible cough, which wracked him to pieces. It was awful to hear him. He couldn't go to work and used to make cloth rugs to try and eke out a living. We were always collecting old trousers and coats for him to use, until he became too ill. He was really slowly dying.

When our gran died, Martha used to come and visit us more often. She always wore a little black bonnet on her head, tied under her chin with a broad black silk ribbon, a short black beaded cape, very shabby and green with age. She had a quivering, tremulous voice and always sounded as if any minute she would burst into tears, but she never did. Poor little pathetic Martha, so very different from her coarse sister - our gran - the only resemblance being the big brown eyes.

6

Round the top of our court were four houses, which were away from the noise of the children and the drunkeness of the men coming home late at night. They were occupied by old people. In the second house was Mrs Greasley, such a sweet old lady, but bedridden with arthritis and stone deaf. She must have been in constant pain, her hands were all swollen and misshapen. Mam used to do a bit of washing for her and the neighbours (including Mrs Trapp) used to empty her commode from time to time. Mrs Greasley stayed in bed all the time in winter to keep warm and only had a few sticks of wood with which to boil a kettle for a cup of tea, as she couldn't afford much coal and was too proud to ask for what she called 'charity coal' and 'parish relief', all she had was 5/- a week old age pension. Her bed was up in the corner under the window, as she couldn't go upstairs.

In the middle of the room was a deal table covered with all sorts of commodities like tea, sugar, condensed milk, bread and margarine, cup and saucer, plate, knife, fork, spoon, a bowl, soap and towel, which she had to rely on the neighbours to give her. There was also a chest of drawers by the wall which contained her clean sheets, towels, etc., which mam used to air for her, as she had no fire. It was very dirty washing, as the sheets were covered in flea marks. On the floor were two cloth rugs made from old coats and trousers. Some days in the summer when the arthritis was not so painful, she would try to get out of bed to what she called 'tidy up' and get clean sheets out of the drawers herself, but on cold, wet days she couldn't move, so had to rely on neighbours, poor Mrs Greasley.

Although Grace was so small, she used to sit and chatter to her (or rather shout at her) and the old lady used to look forward to the child coming. After Grace had been shouting at her for about five minutes, she would hear tap tap tap on the cobbled yard outside and knew it would be old Mrs Smithers, who lived two doors away with her son Joe. Mrs Smithers was nearly blind and had a wooden leg. The children used to shout after her 'Old Granny Peg Leg.' 'Poor old gel,' our mam used to say.

Her son was about thirty, he had married, but his wife had left him so he had come home to live with his poor, blind mother, who couldn't really look after herself. He was an upholsterer and worked at one of the leading furniture shops in the town and sometimes he did repair jobs for our neighbours in his spare time. He would bring an old chair into the yard and with his mouth full of tacks, hammer away fixing the webbing underneath the seat. This used to fascinate Grace who used to watch him at work, tipping his head back as he filled his mouth with tacks, then quickly taking them out one by one. She was always afraid he would forget and swallow some of them and wait for him to gulp, but he never did. He was a sullen sort of chap, never speaking much to anyone. He was short with a ginger moustache like our dad's. He always wore his cap, so nobody knew whether he was bald or not, he even wore it in the house and Grace used to wonder if he wore it in bed. His mother would never grumble at him, if he did, because she couldn't see him properly.

Poor Mrs Smithers used to make an excuse to come and borrow a bit of tea or sugar whenever she heard Grace's voice shouting at Mrs Greasley, to pick up any gossip she might tell her. She had very sharp ears like most blind people. She was unable to go far. her only journeys were to the closet and the water tap, which must have been an ordeal. Her eyes were open, but white with cataracts, which were never removed in those days. She always walked by the wall, using her hands to feel where she was. Sometimes Grace would ask her if she wanted any water fetching, but she would say, 'It's orlight me dear, Joe'll fetch some when 'e coes 'ome.' She was very independent and thought she might have to give her a halfpenny and she couldn't afford that.

She had no teeth and her grey hair was parted down the middle with a wide parting like our gran's, with a knob at the back. She always wore a little black shawl round her shoulders when she came out in the yard.

One day during the next winter, which was a very sharp one, a neighbour found Mrs Greasley stiff with cold. Her lips were blue and she was unable to speak, so she fetched Mrs Trapp who thought the doctor ought to come. Poor Mrs Greasley knew that if he came he would send her to the dreaded workhouse and that would be the end, but she could only use her eyes like a dumb animal, to implore them not to call the doctor. Eventually, however, he had to come and he ordered her removal to the dreaded workhouse, but she only lived a week.

Our mam and Grace cried and so did old Mrs Smithers, who had lost her only friend. Very soon after Mrs Smithers had to go to the workhouse herself, as she had now become quite blind and it was too much for her son Joe, to look after her, as she was not safe to be left alone and he had to go to work. When any of the neighbours went to see her she would implore them to take her home. She didn't live long after that. 'Poor old gel,' as our mam used to say. The old people were terrified of the threat of the workhouse in those days, as they knew when they went there it was really the end.

7

One night, a night we never forgot, we were huddled together waiting for our dad to come home from the pub. Mam used to keep us up late for company, because she was always scared of him when he was drunk. This particular night was a Friday night and 'The Greyhound' didn't close until 11pm that night. Grace always had instructions to run down the street and find a policeman if he started knocking mam about. The policemen always walked about in pairs in our district.

The old clock on the wall, with its pendulum swinging backwards and forwards rhythmically, making a loud tick tock, tick tock, suddenly made a whizzing noise and clanged out 11 o'clock. We clung together in the darkest corner of the room, away from the firelight, listening to the voices of the men turning out of the pub and the footsteps of our dad on the cobblestones of the yard. We heard, 'Goodnight Sam.' 'Goodnight Ted,' (our dad). Then a lot of laughter, followed by, 'Yo wait till yo gerome wi' 'im, Ted.' They were all arguing and fighting one another. Then his uncertain footsteps coming up the yard.

'Ush,' said mam in an awed voice, 'E's got somebody with 'im. 'E's talking to somebody. Oh dear what shall we do? ' We held our breath, trembling all over as we listened and waited. So terrified now, as we knew something dreadful was going to happen. Grace started to whimper.

'Shut up, it's no good blartin',' mam said, but she must have been very near to tears herself. He had been inside that pub all the evening, three or four hours drinking, so he must be in a drunken state by now. The beer seemed to be double strength in those days and the effect it had on all the occupants of that court seemed to our childish imagination to make them into terrifying monsters.

Clip clop, clip clop, came his footsteps, nearer and nearer to our door. He always knew which was the right door even though he was blind drunk and all the houses in the court were the same.

'Come on, yo bugger come on,' he was saying. Suddenly the latch lifted and in he stumbled and from the dim light of the paraffin lamp on the table in the middle of the room, we saw to our amusement and our mam's horror, that he had an animal with him on a lead.

'Oh my God,' said mam, as the thing went Mrrrrr-----Mrrrrr, 'It ain't a dog, it's a nanny goat,' and he was bringing it into our one and only living room. When mam recovered from her fright and found her voice, she yelled, 'Whatever 'ave yer got theere? It ain't coming in 'ere.'

Dad reeled and staggered into the table, the poor goat going with him holding it's head down, Mrrrrr----ing and charging. The table rocked, nearly knocking the paraffin lamp over and scaring us all to death. Grace and I started screaming. He was so drunk he kept laughing and saying,

'E's coming upstairs to bed wi' me for a change, ha ha ha,' and before mam could stop him, he opened the stairs door and was stumbling up the stairs dragging the goat with him. It was Mrrrr---ing all the way.

Mam started crying herself, but he was by now staggering about in the room above, having climbed the stairs somehow and was trying to find the candle to light it, cursing and swearing because he couldn't find it. To crown it all our gran came in from the pub bringing her half-pint in a jug, laughing and jeering. She was also drunk as somebody had treated her to an extra pint as it was Friday night. She had seen him win the goat with a raffle ticket and she knew what mam would say when he took it home. How they hated one another. Gran enjoyed crowing over her not being able to stop him taking it upstairs to bed with him.

'Gew and light the bloody candle fer 'im, else he'll break 'is bloody neck,' she yelled. 'But that's what yo wan' ain't it, yo bitch.'

Our poor, unhappy mam, she was torn between desire to help him in case he did fall down and hurt himself and doing what gran had told her to do, whom she hated, the feeling being mutual. Finally for our sakes, she reluctantly dragged herself up the stairs with a lighted candle, crying as she went.

'Gerra bloody move on can't yet,' he shouted when mam reached the top of the stairs. She could see him slumped over in the corner of the room, pulling the poor animal, who was Mrrr---ing away. Out of the room were more stairs leading up to the attic room and suddenly mam had an idea, or was it an answer to a prayer, as she had been silently praying to herself all the time

She realised that she had the whip hand because she had the lighted candle in her hand and he couldn't see where he was without it. So up the rickety stairs to the attic room went mam, shouting to him over her shoulder, 'Come on,' and to our amazement he scrambled to his feet, pulling the goat after him towards the second flight of stairs.

'Bring the animal up 'ere,' she shouted again. We were peering up the stairs through the open door, but when he moved we scuttled away in case he came our way head first down the first flight of stairs. We heard with relief, him stumbling up the second lot of stairs after our mam and the light, but we were frightened in case he turned on her. She knew it was no good arguing with him in that drunken state, but she did say to him.

'Bringin' that 'orrible animal up 'ere. What about the smell?'

He said, 'Oh he'll 'ave ter get used to that, wone 'er,' and laughted. 'The smell, that's a good 'un, ha ha ha.' Listening below, we thought he would never stop laughing. Mam set the lighted candle high up on the mantle shelf out of his reach, standing on a chair to do so. Then she pushed past him, leaving him still laughing about the smell and ran down the two flights of stairs at a gallop, pushing us away from the door at the bottom.

'Come on now, you get ready for bed, it is past midnight, you must sleep wi' me tonight and we must lock the bedroom door.'

She looked across to where gran was sitting by the fire stirring her beer with a red-hot poker, chuckling away to herself, thinking how she had scored over mam, but not knowing that when she went to bed, she would have to share the room with our dad and the goat, and not our mam. We would be safe in mam's room and we could do all the chuckling then when she went to bed, if we were still awake. But we were very tired and went straight to sleep, huddled together in the big bed. After about an hour, we were awakened by a lot of banging and shouting and we all knew our gran had found out about our dad and the goat. Poor mam, she would suffer for this.

Next morning we could hear movements in the attic room above, as soon as it was daylight and wondered what that animal looked like. But we daren't open the bedroom door as we were alone, mam having gone down early to wait for our dad. She had hardly slept a wink. At last we heard him go downstairs, the poor goat still Mrrr--ing away. Then we heard loud words from mam as soon as he opened the door. She shouted at the top of her voice, 'Yo' can tek that stinking thing out of 'ere, it ain't having a bite in this 'ouse.'

Dad never answered her back, he was sober now. He quietly opened the door and went down the yard, dragging the poor animal with him. It must have been very hungry now. When our dad was sober, he was a different personality altogether, quiet and shy. Mam was the domineering one. In about half an hour he came back without the goat, having sold it for 1/-, or so he said, to one of his mates. It looked as if he had learned his lesson, but it was short lived, as the next pay day found him again in the pub, spending nearly all his wages, treating everybody. This meant another visit to 'uncle's' on Monday morning, so mam could get some money to buy the food we needed.

Sometimes she wished he would join the army like some of the other men in the street. She would have a bit of peace. The money was poor, but regular. They only got 1/- a day then. Whenever they had a row he was always threatening to join, but he was a short man and knew he wouldn't be tall enough. So mam had to put up with his drunken habits as well as our gran's.

Lots of his mates had allotments in the park, as in the courts they had no back door let alone a garden and it was a common sight to see them trundling their little trucks along the street full of vegetables and flowers, which they sold in the pub for a pint or two. The outskirts of Coventry were full of allotments then. Sweet Williams were the favourite flowers and even to this day they remind me of that pub, especially the striped ones. Everybody in those days seemed to be struggling to earn a copper somehow. There was the knife grinder and scissor sharpener with his barrow. There were the Russian bears on chains, usually dancing to a mouth-organ, played by one man, another holding out his can for coppers. The German brass band, with four or five men playing different instruments and another man collecting when the crowd gathered around. The tramp singing *Rock of Ages* or *Abide With Me* (evading the policeman), while we, feeling sorry for him, would give him the farthing we were saving to spend on sweets. Then along would come the hurdy gurdy with a little monkey on top, dressed in a bright red coat to keep him warm. How we loved that monkey, as the man would feed him with nuts. To our amusement the monkey would sit there taking the shells off the nuts while the handle was turned to churn out the reportoire of music like *Goodbye Dolly Grey, Come into the Garden Maud, Alice Where Art Thou* and lots more favourites of the day. We all stood fascinated, when the monkey finishing his nuts, he would come down from the top of the barrel-organ with a long cord attached to a collar round his neck and jump about amongst the crowd, the children shrieking with laughter at its antics. A cap would be placed on top of the organ for the money when all the tunes had been played. There always seemed to be plenty of coppers in the cap, as this was the biggest attraction of all the street entertainers. The monkey would then jump on top again and off they would go into the next street to play the tunes all over again. Sometimes, forgetting the time, we would follow and so would lots more children. The hurdy gurdy was often the cause of the cane being used for the latecomers at school. It was such an attraction to the children of all ages.

We had very little money, but we did enjoy all the fun. We often went hungry, but everybody was poor and we shared what little we had with one another. We played games such as five-stones which we collected, and hopscotch with a stone and a piece of chalk.

The next big attraction was the rag and bone man, shouting out, 'Any old rags or bones,' with coloured balloons all festooned over his cart and goldfish in jars of water, in exchange for bundles of rags and the best woollens. We would dash up the yard and into the house for a few rags, woollens or rabbit skins, to get a balloon or a jar of goldfish. Our mam would shout, 'Gew on wi' yet. I 'eard 'im. I ain't gorany rags for him.'

But we would say, 'Oh gew on Mam.'

'Oh yor' a nuisance. I ain't gorany, I tell yer.' But somehow she managed to find some odds and ends after ransacking all the drawers and as we ran down the yard Mrs Trapp would shout, 'Ere yar both on yer, tak 'im these,' throwing us a bundle of rags and off we would race so excited, to the rag and bone man, still shouting further down the street, with children running in and out of doors and courts with small bundles in their arms. But the goldfish in the glass jars always seemed to stay on his cart. Without looking to see what each child had brought, he would give them a balloon. Goodness knows what he required for a goldfish. Mam said he was a twister and never gave them away, even if you gave a new suit, which was probably right.

8

All the dustbins belonging to the houses in the court were kept in the back yard by the side of the closets, and our Grace sometimes used to see half dead flowers hanging out of one of the bins. She loved flowers and tried to get a bunch to give mam for her birthday, as she couldn't buy her any, having no money of her own. Poor Grace, she thought she was giving mam such a nice surprise when she gave her a few flowers on her birthday. Mam pretended to be pleased with them, but she wondered where they had come from, as they weren't all that fresh, but she didn't ask any questions, because she thought it was such a nice gesture.

About a week after mam's birthday, Grace woke up one morning with a high temperature and a sore throat. Mam was a bit worried in case she got worse and would have to have a doctor, because our dispensary club was in arrears. A collector used to call on a Monday and sometimes mam hadn't got the fourpence subscription. The last time the man called he said, 'If you don't pay next time I call missus, I shall have to report you and you might be struck off the books, then no doctor would call if needed.' Poor mam looked round to see what she could take to the pawnshop to get a few coppers and all she could think of was her only pair of brown shoes, her Sunday best. She wrapped them up in a piece of paper and told me to run down to the pawnshop and get a customer in the shop to ask Mr Samuels for 1/- for them, as I wasn't old enough to pawn.

Off I went, running all the way there, but I could only get 8d. Mam said, 'Well I suppose that'll have to do for now. But 'e needn't think 'e is goin' to 'ave me best Sunday shoes for 8d, the twister. I'll get 'em back somehow.' She then sent me to the dispensary in Priory Street with the 8d in case Grace got worse and we needed a doctor, which we did.

Next morning Grace was delirious (light headed as mam called it) tossing about on the bed, hot as fire, rambling away. The doctor had to be sent for. There were two doctors allocated to Much Park Street and St. John's Street, Dr. Lamb and Dr. Pitt. Dr Lamb was a very sharp tongued man, contrary to his name and mam was afraid if he knew the book wasn't straight, he would refuse to come. Dr. Pitt was just the opposite. He was a very nicely spoken, gentle little man, whom everybody loved, but sure enough it was Dr. Lamb who called.

Grace lay on the sofa in our one and only room, tossing her head from side to side on the pillow, her face still the colour of a tomato and not answering mam when she spoke to her. Poor mam was nearly out of her mind with worry and she cried and begged Grace to answer her, knowing in her heart that she was gravely ill. She kept saying, 'Grace, speak to me please, please speak to me. I'll never shout at yet agin, I won't and I'll work me fingers to the bone for yet, if yet will only speak to me.' The tears running down her face, but Grace couldn't hear her, she was too ill.

When Dr. Lamb did come, he walked straight in without knocking, leaving the door wide open and went straight over to the table where the dispensary book was, putting on his spectacles to look at the subscriptions entered before he even looked at our Grace. Mam went over and shut the door. The eight pence I had taken to the dispensary wasn't enough to cancel all the arrears, but it helped. He looked at the book, then looked over his glasses at Grace lying there on the sofa. She was making a strange gurgling noise in her throat, but he still stood by the table with the book in his hand.

'For God's sake doctor, do something,' sobbed mam, but he shut the book and just said, 'In future keep up your subscriptions.'

Going over to the sofa, he shouted, 'Open your mouth child,' but Grace took no notice of him, so he said to mam, 'Hold her head woman.' Mam tremblingly did as she was told, then he forced Grace's mouth open and shone a little lamp down her throat.

There was a minute's silence, which seemed like an hour, then as if suddenly making up his mind, he said, 'Good God woman, she's got diphtheria. You must paint her throat every hour. It must be got clear in twenty-four hours or she will die. Send to the surgery at once for the necessary prescription, which will be 5/- and that doesn't come off the club, as it is very expensive.'

Poor mam was all agitated and at her wit's end, as this meant another visit to the pawnshop, but what could she take this time to provide 5/-? All she could think of was the bedclothes, blankets and sheets off her own bed. She would have to put all our coats on until she could do enough washing and charring to redeem them. She went upstairs and tore the clothes off the bed and ran down the street into the pawnshop, going herself this time, leaving Mrs Trapp to watch Grace, as she had got to make 'old Samuels' give her 5/- for the things she had brought. She told him it was a matter of life and death and implored him to give her the money, but he was a hard-hearted man and was used to listening to hard luck stories, but at last, after much pleading he relented.

She snatched the money and rushed out of the shop, with it clasped tight in her hand and ran along home. Mrs Trapp couldn't stay any longer with Grace, as she had to get a meal ready for all her family, so mam had to let me go to the surgery. She tied the money (two precious half-crowns), in a handkerchief and gave me strict instructions to hold it tight.

I ran all the way to the surgery in Cox Street, quite a distance from where we lived in Much Park Street. The doctor had said to knock on the front door, not to wait in the surgery and as we were so very poor and I wasn't very old, I felt very proud, as only private patients were allowed through the front door. A servant girl came to the door and when I told her what I wanted, she reached over to a shelf to get the package, but she had been instructed by the doctor not to give it to me unless I had got the 5/-. She said, 'Where is the money?' and I gave her the knotted handkerchief with the two half-crowns in, without undoing it. She undid it, took

24

out the money, gave me my handkerchief back and the precious stuff to paint Grace's throat with. I held it tightly in my hand and ran off home as fast as my little legs could carry me. I loved Grace and didn't want her to die and the doctor said she would if we didn't paint her throat quickly.

When I got home mam snatched the bottle from me. It was only a small bottle and had a little brush tied on to the side of it, to brush her throat with, but somebody had got to hold her head still so that mam could force her mouth open and I wasn't old enough. She said, 'Fetch Mrs Trapp quick.' So down the yard I ran again and banged on Mrs Trapp's door. When she opened it, I blurted out, 'Mam says come quick.' Up she came at once, dropping everything she was doing, such a good heart she had. Her very presence so comforting and she loved our Grace.

I stood there whimpering and trembling while both of them tried to wrench her mouth open, but Grace kept her lips tightly closed. She wouldn't open her mouth even for Mrs Trapp. Poor mam cried and wrung her hands, 'Whatever shall we do?' she wailed.

Mrs Trapp said, 'Go an' fetch that theer doctor agin, we're wastin' time, she'll 'ave to open 'er mouth for 'im. He'll mek'er, gew on run missus, quick,' so mam snatched her coat off the nail on the door and ran all the way to the surgery. She knocked on the front door of the house regardless of 'For Private Patients only' marked on it. The same servant girl answered and said,

'What do you want at this door, can't you read? This door is for private patients only,' recognising mam as having been to the surgery.

'I want to see the doctor straight away. He must come at once, my child is dying with diphtheria,' mam said, crying hysterically.

The girl said, 'You must take your turn in the surgery like all the rest,' but mam pushed her on one side and before she could stop her or call out, she pushed past her and ran into the door marked 'Private', which was the doctor's room. The doctor was too surprised to be angry when he saw what a state she was in and she blurted out,

'She won't let me paint her throat. I can't open her mouth. Oh! whatever shall I do, for God's sake come now, come I implore you Doctor or it will be too late. Oh! Dr Lamb have pity on us.' Screaming out his name, disregarding the patient who was sitting facing him at the table.

The doctor was a very hard man and he stared at her for a second, then he said, 'Control yourself woman. I will send the District Nurse. Can't you see I am busy. Your daughter isn't the only patient I have got on my books, you know.'

Poor mam beside herself with grief just stood and stared at him, her mouth twitching, while he tore a piece of paper off his pad and scribbled the nurse's name and address on it, handing it to her across the table. She snatched it out of his hand running out of the room and out of the house, letting herself out of that front door. Hardly believing anyone could be so cruel, sobbing as she went down the street, scarcely knowing which direction to take for the quickest. Passers-by stopped and stared after her, but she saw nobody.

The district nurses all lived together in a house in Manor Road, a small road off Park Road, which was by the railway station, quite a distance from the surgery in Cox Street. It took her about fifteen minutes running all the way. As she got nearer to Manor Road she took the piece of paper out of her pocket and by the light of the street lamp read the nurse's name and the number of the house she wanted. After going through one or two garden gates and peering at the numbers on the doors, she found the one she was looking for.

Another servant girl answered the door and mam said, 'Is Nurse Wilson in please,' all out of breath through running, holding out the piece of paper to the girl, who took it further into the hall to read it under the gas light (here they had gas not paraffin lamps like us). Coming back to mam standing in the doorway, she said, 'It is very late, Nurse Wilson is just going to bed.'

'Never mind that my child is dying,' said mam and moved forward to go further into the hall, but the girl put out her hand and said, 'Just a minute please, I will take the message to the nurse, if you will wait here,' in a kinder voice altogether from the other servant girl at the doctor's house.

After about five minutes, which seemed like a lifetime to mam listening to the grandfather clock ticking away in the corner, Nurse Wilson herself came slowly down the stairs in front of her. Mam rushed forward and cried, 'Oh! Nurse please 'urry, my child has got diphtheria and won't let us paint 'er throat. She is dying I tell yet. Oh! Do please come now,' in such a tearful, pleading voice that the nurse who was a kind type of woman said,' Now dear, don't upset yourself. I will come. Where did you say you lived, Much Park Street? Oh! That won't take me long on my bicycle. Just give me the number of the court and the house and I will be there before you are, if I start right away.' Which she did. She could see that mam's distress was genuine and knew how urgent it was to get that throat cleared as quickly as possible if the child was to live.

When mam got back home, running all the way again, gasping for breath, the nurse was already there, she had taken her coat off and was warming her hands by the fire as it was a very cold night, but mam hadn't noticed it. Going over to the sofa where Grace lay, still tossing her head on the pillow, she said to Mrs Trapp, who had stayed with us while mam had been away, 'Now will you hold her head as firmly as you can while I try and open her mouth.'

Mrs Trapp got at the back of her and held her head firmly in both hands and the nurse said to Grace, 'Now dear, open your mouth, there's a good little girl.' To everybody's amazement, she opened her mouth wide. It was as if an angel had come into the room, it was so wonderful.

'Now somebody please pass the bottle and brush,' said the nurse, 'Keep your mouth open dear, I promise I won't hurt you at all.'

She painted Grace's throat just in the nick of time. She stayed all the night and came every few hours during the day until the danger had passed. How we all loved that nurse, as our Grace would certainly have died if mam hadn't run about like she did and if the nurse hadn't acted so quickly. Poor mam was so exhausted, but so relieved when Grace let the nurse paint her throat, that for the first time in her life, she knelt on the stone floor and thanked God for hearing her prayer, as she had been praying as she had been running all that way, first to the doctor and then to the nurse.

Our house was No.7 and at No.10 little Jimmy Whitehead died with diphtheria the next day. He was only three years old and such a pretty little boy with fair curls all over his head. His mother and father were brokenhearted.

Grace was ill for seven weeks and lay on the sofa looking like a ghost. Mam had to teach her to walk again, as diphtheria is accompanied by a sort of paralysis of the legs. I was glad when she could come upstairs again as I had missed her so much. I missed the fairy stories we used to tell each other when we were tucked up in bed, about beautiful princesses and handsome princes. Our gran had a single bed in the corner of the room, but she was so deaf and sometimes so drunk, she couldn't hear us.

Mam hadn't had much schooling, but she had plenty of common sense and courage and when Grace was well again she made up her mind to get us out of that court somehow, with all its smells and drunken quarrels. Our dad was upset when Grace was so ill, but he was content to stay there in that environment, as he had been born there and brought up in it, but not our mam.

9

On the corner of our street was a draper's shop where our mam used to take us sometimes to buy some of our clothes, using vouchers from a weekly club. It was a friendly shop where you could wander in and out of the various departments, going down a sort of ramp from one room to another, then up some narrow stairs to the millinery department, trying on hats with no interference from the assistants. We all loved to go into this shop. It had windows and entrances in both Jordan Well and Much Park Street. On the other corner was an undertaker's shop displaying numerous artificial wreaths encased in domed glass covers with appropriate inscriptions inside, engraved on a white celluloid strip.

Just round the corner was a chemist shop, which had a notice displayed in the window, 'Teeth Extracted, Sixpence'. As Grace was always crying with the toothache and keeping us awake at night, mam decided she had got to have the tooth out. As there was no anaesthetic given for teeth extraction then (at least not for the likes of us), it was a very painful affair and all sorts of remedies, or so called remedies, were used to avoid having the tooth out. I can remember mam dragging poor Grace into the shop and saying to the old man behind the counter, 'We want a

27

tooth taking out please.' He was an old man with a long white beard and steel-rimmed spectacles halfway down his nose.

When he had finished serving his customer he shuffled into a room at the back of the shop, beckoned us to follow, muttering to Grace who was whimpering, 'Sit down, open your mouth, which one is it?' all in one breath. Mam pointed to the troublesome tooth and he produced some pincers from a pocket at the back of his coat. At this point I dashed out of the shop and stood further along the street waiting for Grace to yell, and yell she did. I thought he was pulling her head off. We were a long time before we dared to go into that shop again and when we had to go by, we fairly ran by. The chemist shops in those days had three large bottles in the window with coloured water in them, red, blue and green. The bottles had pointed glass stoppers. There was no other window display and you just dashed in and out again as quickly as possible.

Sometimes mam used to take us to see our other gran (her mother), who lived in a little house at the bottom of Hill Top, which was a little cobbled lane going off Priory Row, where Earl Leofric and Lady Godiva once lived. There was also a Blue Coat charity school for girls there, which opened in 1714 and was rebuilt on the same site in 1856. This gran was a very nice kind old lady, so different from our other gran. She had rosy, sunken cheeks, no teeth and snow white hair. She had the same blue eyes as our mam, which twinkled like little stars when she laughed. She always wore a tight fitting black bodice, well nearly green, as it was very shabby, the collar fastening high in her neck, nearly reaching her ears. She was very poor like the rest of us. Her husband, our grandpa, had been dead for a number of years, having died of consumption. She had been left with seven children to bring up somehow. She had to go out washing and charing. She was always changing houses because of the rent. If she saw a house a shilling cheaper, she would get one of her sons (now all married) to hire a hand cart to move her goods and chattels.

There were five sons, a drunken lot, our mam and Aunt Jennie. Poor Aunt Jennie was always crying. She had been jilted when she was very young and deeply in love and never got over it, although now married. She was very quiet and unhappy. How gran lived was a mystery, as what money the sons earned had to go to their own families. They would sometimes drop her a shilling every now and then if it hadn't all gone on beer.

We used to like to visit her as she was so cheerful and though she was so poor there was always a good fire, banked up with slack, filling the room up with smoke. When she saw us coming she would give it a good poke, leaving the poker in and making more smoke, then after a minute or two it would burst into flames. Then she would put on the old black kettle off the hob for a cup of tea. She would put the cups without saucers on a tin tray, ready on the table. In the corner by the smoky fire sat a very old man in an upright wooden armchair. He had a long, grubby beard, which to our amusement went up and down when he ate and drank

28

his tea. He had no teeth, so when he sucked in his tea his moustache was drawn in with it. His legs were covered by a piece of old grey blanket. He must have been paralysed as he never moved and never seemed to speak to anybody. He was always referred to as Uncle Ned. What relation he was to gran we never knew, but perhaps he was the answer to the mystery of how she lived. He may have been the lodger.

To get to gran's house we went up Earl Street, past the Palace Yard, full of medieval buildings, crossed the road to Hay Lane, along Cuckoo Lane into Priory Row and down Hill Top. After we had all had a cup of tea, it was time to go home and we went back a different way, because mam liked to get something tasty for our dad's tea. We went up New Buildings, past the ragged school into Ironmonger Row, passed the rag and bone men taking their wares down Palmer Lane, which went off Ironmonger Row and Cross Cheaping. We went up Butcher Row, which had quaint antique shops, secondhand bookshops, wardrobe dealers, etc., with their goods displayed on the pavement outside the shops. The buildings were half-timbered with the top half jutting out over the lower half. The windows upstairs were latticed. The street was narrow and cobbled.

Halfway down was a shop where they sold pig's trotters and peas at 4d for the trotters and 2d for a saucer of peas. On the corner was a fishmonger's shop, where a man would shout out selling his fish, getting pieces of plaice, cod, etc., out of a bucket of cold water, slapping them onto a marble slab at the front of the shop. He used to wear a straw brimmer and a navy and white striped apron. Winter or summer he was there, swilling down the slabs with cold water after all the fish had been sold. Mam bought a small piece of cod for 3d for our dad's tea.

We then turned into Trinity Churchyard. We would have liked to go into Broadgate where the tram terminus was, so that we could watch the driver get out of the tram and fix the trolley pole on to the wires overhead, making a spark, before starting off again in the direction of Smithford Street, which was a narrow street with double lines, but mam said no, we would be late for dad's tea. We went through Pepper Lane, where the tops of the tiny houses nearly touched each other across the narrow street. Parallel with Pepper Lane was a funny little lane called Derby Lane with one or two tiny little houses. At the end of Pepper Lane, on the corner was 'The Golden Cross' public house, which was 500 years old. This time we went straight on down Bayley Lane, past St. Michael's Church and St. Mary's Hall and the Police Station into St. Mary's Street. On the corner of this street was a large draper's shop, which had two windows in Earl Street and two in St Mary's Street, with an entrance in each street. We rarely went into this shop because it was rather select and we couldn't afford their prices. Sometimes mam wanted a yard of ribbon or lace, so we ventured in with her, but never on our own.

I can see the inside of that shop now. There was a counter on each side with lady assistants standing there waiting to serve. There was a row of chairs in front of each counter for customers to sit, after they had asked for whatever they wished to purchase. As soon as a customer entered the shop, the shopwalker would come forward and bowing politely, ask what was required. He would then direct them to the appropriate counter. He usually wore a white bow tie, swallow tail coat and striped trousers. Should the goods required not be in stock, the assistant was obliged to signal the shopwalker. He would be waiting to be called to the counter to sign and check the amount charged for the goods purchased. When the assistant explained to him the difficulty in satisfying the customer, he would try to persuade them to purchase something else. It was always a terrible job to get out of the shop without making a purchase. The assistant was regarded as most incompetent by the management if this happened.

We were now almost home and had only to cross the road and turn into Much Park Street. We would usually run on in front to lay the table for tea, so as to get out quickly to play in the brewery yard before it got dark, but before doing this mam would shout for us to get our good clothes off before we went.

10

Going 'up the town' on a Saturday night was a treat we always looked forward to as there was so much to see. This only happened if our dad was sober and had a spare shilling in his pocket, which he had won gambling. We used to watch him get ready to go to the pub as usual and if he said, 'Come on, I'll tek yo two up the tahn ter see the shops if yo 'urry up and git ready.' We would be so excited and really hurry.

On the street corners would be the paper boy selling papers, shouting something which seemed to be in a foreign language. With a folded paper in his outstretched hand he would push it into people's faces to try and sell out as quickly as possible, especially if it was wintertime. In the market square were the street traders, the chestnut sellers, selling a pennyworth of hot chestnuts from his brazier, the hot potato man with his barrow carrying an oven with a glowing fire underneath, a little sack of coal on the front of the barrow. All round the top of the oven were spikes on which were impaled potatoes in their jackets. The man shouted, '2d for four,' and in the summertime there was the ice-cream man. Everybody shouted one against the other like, 'Ripe bananas two a penny, oranges two a penny, rosy apples 2d a pound,' etc. The stalls were lit with naphtha lamps, the 'quacks' guaranteeing their medicine and pills to cure every ache and pain.

If I remember rightly there were three pubs in this square, 'The Hole in the Wall', next door to a fishmonger's shop, 'The Market Tavern' and 'The Dolphin'. Leading out of the square was a covered market hall with a clock on a tower, with faces on all four sides. On Saturday nights the butchers auctioned their meat. They kept open until 11pm and people waited hours for pieces of beef, which they got for 1/- and 1/6d. The Market Hall was a very attractive place at Christmastime.

There were Chinese lanterns and paper-chains festooned across from one stall to another with 'Merry Christmas' spelt out in gold letters and Father Christmas with a bran tub and lucky dips.

After we had been to the market, our dad would take us 'Round the tahn' as he called it, buying us a toy from the 6d bazaar down Smithford Street and sometimes taking us to the railway station to see the trains come in. We loved that. It was so exciting seeing an express rushing through the station, making such a deafening noise. When a train did stop the porters shouted, 'Coventry, all change,' opening and shutting (or banging) all the carriage doors and the guard waved a little green flag and blew a whistle when it was time for the train to go out again. Outside the station there were the bootblacks, shining shoes for a few coppers and a line of hansom cabs waiting to pick up passengers and their luggage and take them wherever they wanted to go.

To get to the station, which was in Eaton Road, we went down Hertford Street, past a pub called 'The Peeping Tom', with a figure looking out of an upstairs window. We were both very interested in this figure, because he had no eyes and we wanted to know why. Our dad told us it was because he was supposed to have peeped at Lady Godiva when she rode round the streets of Coventry hundreds of years ago, without any clothes, mounted on a beautiful white horse, to remove the taxes put upon the people by her husband Earl Leofric. She had said she would ride naked on condition everybody kept indoors with the windows and doors barred, which they did, except Peeping Tom, but he was struck blind before he could see her.

We loved these jaunts with our dad, but they were few and far between. He used to take us such a long way making us so tired I used to cry, so he had to carry me. When he was away from the pub, his pals and our gran, he was a different man. When we told mam how kind he had been carrying me because I was tired, she grumbled at him for taking us too far, but at the same time she began to puzzle and plan a way to get him and us out of that court. She knew he would never leave his mother. She would always have to come with us wherever we went, which was a big problem for mam.

There was a little shop in Silver Street where they sold faggots and peas, which attracted our dad and some Saturdays he would take us there. Everybody sat on high stools up to the counter and steaming hot peas were put on little saucers. We only had peas, as we didn't like faggots. To get to Silver Street we would go straight up High Street, through Broadgate, down Cross Cheaping and The Burges, passing Hales Street where the Opera House was. Silver Street was just inside Bishop Street, opposite Well Street. The pig market was at the end of the street, which went into Cook Street, where the old city gate is. Both streets were full of pubs and courts and of course a pawnshop. Going through Cook Street we came out in Chauntry Place by the side of the Hippodrome, where there were some

31

more poor little houses. Opposite was the fire station and we were just in time to see the fire engine coming out, bells ringing, horses rearing. There were four horses as far as I can remember. Great excitement, the fireman standing upon the platform, everyone watching to see which way they went. Our dad was itching to follow, but we were much too tired and wanted to go home.

Our dad loved his Coventry and knew it like the back of his hand. He knew the history and story of Lady Godiva and knew where all the city gates were, Gosford Gate, Swanswell Gate, Cook Street Gate, Whitefriars Gate and Spon Gate. He loved to take us to see a Godiva Procession. He was as excited as we were on hearing the bands playing.

There was always great excitement at general election time, especially when the result of the poll was announced. This was delclared by the Mayor from a balcony at the 'King's Head' hotel at midnight. This was at the corner of Hertford Street in Broadgate. All Coventry seemed to turn out for the results to come through. We weren't allowed to sit up, but I can remember hearing the story of how our mam fainted and had to be held up so as not to be trampled on by the crowd. There were always lots of casualties. Everybody went mad and the police on horseback had to take control.

11

About that time there came into the pub at the bottom of our court, a mysterious visitor not known in the district. All the locals looked at one another when he came through the door into the bar and went straight up to the counter, whispering to each other, but no one seemed to know who he was. The landlord was equally puzzled. Usually he knew every one of his customers, as they were there every night of the week. They spent most of their money there and had precious little to take home to their wives on a Friday when they paid for the beer they had had 'on the slate' during the week. Their homes were comfortless places and the pubs only a shade better, with sawdust and spittoons on the floor and small tables with iron legs and wooden forms to sit on, but they liked the company they met there.

The young man who had just entered was obviously not their class although he dressed like them with a cloth cap and a muffler round his neck. He had fair hair and blue eyes, quite a good looker, they said. He was about thirty years of age and about 5' 8" tall and when he ordered his pint of bitter he spoke in a cultured voice. Picking up the beer he went and sat down at one of the tables amongst the other men, looking round as he did so at the inquisitive faces of the regulars. The general hubbub of the bar ceased and it was uncannily quiet for 'The Greyhound'. Everybody seemed to be expecting trouble, the landlord looked uneasy too, but the young man just said, 'Good evening, gentlemen,' in such a quiet, pleasant voice, smiling as he did so and it sounded as if everyone answered, 'Good evening,' back. He stayed for about an hour, chatting to one and another on general topics, such as the weather, the price of a pint, racing and all the subjects that go with a pub, then left as suddenly as he had come saying, 'Well, good evening gentlemen, I must be off.'

When he had gone there was a general discussion as to who he could be and where he came from. Nobody had a clue except the landlord and he had an idea he had seen him in one of the local shops in the town, having an argument with a shopkeeper over the price of an article he wanted to purchase and he was wearing a clerical collar.

On Saturday evening the bar was full to overflowing, everybody talking at once and as the beer flowed so the talk got louder. About 8o'clock the stranger came in again and this time the landlord had no doubt he was the same person he had seen in the shop. He wasn't there on the Sunday, but on Monday he was there again chatting away on all sorts of subjects over his one pint of bitter, getting quite friendly with the men. After he had gone, they began to argue amongst themselves as to who he might be, as he had what they called a 'toff's' voice. They thought perhaps he was one of the actors from the Opera House, rehearsing his part as a working man and getting to know their ways. This went on until Wednesday night and by now they were all curious and stopped talking to stare at him when he came in again. The landlord was very amused, as by now he was quite sure he was a parson and wondered what he was up to, but his money was as good as the rest, so why worry, he thought.

After the young man left there was a heated discussion amongst one or two of the men, our dad included. His pal, Sam Tomms, was older than he was. He had a beard, which always reminded us of Father Christmas. When he had a couple of pints he got very excited and was inclined to quarrel. This particular night our dad had consumed more than enough and was all ready for an argument. After a while he bet Sam a pint that he daren't ask the man if he was a parson. He didn't dare ask himself and knew that old Sam couldn't resist a free pint.

'Who darsen', I'll arsk 'im I know,' said old Sam, with a vision of a free pint before his eyes, but the young man did not come again until Friday. By this time old Sam's courage had begun to fail and he whispered to dad, 'Ere, I reckon 'e ain't no parson, 'e's a bloody actor.'

'No 'e ain't,' the others shouted, overhearing what he said. 'Yo's backin' aht. Yo darsen arsk 'im.'

When the young man walked through the door, all eyes turned to look at Sam. The bar was full and it couldn't have been a better night for a parson. Sam waited until he was well and truly oiled, then full of beer courage, he sauntered up to the young man, who was sitting talking to one of Sam's mates. Everyone was watching, but our dad kept well in the rear, he wasn't the pushing sort. This was the very moment the parson had waited for so patiently all this time. He knew full well what was in the men's minds and that sooner or later one of them would have the courage to ask him who he was, so he was ready.

When Sam finally got up to him, he went straight to the point, having rehearsed his little piece over and over again to himself. He blurted out quick like, 'Oi, is it true yore a parson and if it is wot yo doin' in 'ere? Yo oughter be in church, that's yore proper place. And wheer's that theer dog collar yore supposed ter weer. Yove no business wi' that theer cap on.' Sam stopped to get his breath after that long speech.

The young man was by now on friendly terms with all the men, calling them all by their Christian names. As they stopped talking and were watching and waiting for his answer, he said, standing up with his pint in one hand looking round the bar. 'Well Sam it's quite true, I am a parson.' He whipped off his muffler revealing a dog collar. 'If you would rather I came in here with this showing, well that's all right by me. If you chaps don't mind that is.'

'Well wot abaht that theer pint yo'm 'aving?' said Sam, for something to say.

'Well, what about it? I've paid for it the same as you, haven't I?' said the parson.

Well old Sam didn't know what to say after that and went all quiet like, feeling a proper fool with everybody in the bar staring at him. Our dad came to the rescue and said, 'Well Sam youm won yor pint, 'ere tis.'

The parson seizing his opportunity said, 'What's this you say. He has actually won a pint just by asking me if I am a parson. Well, well, I will stand another pint all round, that you daren't come to my church and hear me preach next Sunday.'

At this there was a roar of laughter and they said, 'Ah, we'll come for a pint, by God we will.'

As quick as lightening, he took them up on it, 'Righto chaps, that's a deal. I'll find you all special seats in the back row of the gallery. I'll be at Christ Church door at 6.15pm. The service starts at 6.30pm. Now don't let me down, or no pint on Monday night,' and with that he went out of the door, chuckling to himself all down the street, having won the first round all right and feeling sure they would come because of the free pint.

After he had gone out of the pub the bar was quiet for a few minutes, old Sam coughing and spitting into the sawdust on the floor to hide his agitation. Then up jumped Tom Birch, a thin, scraggy little man with small beady eyes and ginger hair, who looked as if a square meal would do him good. 'Well yo'm gorn and don it naw, but I'll gew for a lark and a free pint if yo will,' he said.

Our dad, also full of beer, said, 'Well we all promised the bloke we'd gew, so I suppose we'll bloody well ha'to.'

'Will yer, Ted?' says Tommy.

'So will I,' said George Mills. A big burly, bully of a chap, all punches and curses, about 6ft tall, who everybody was afraid of. 'If it's only to get that bloody pint.'

So it was unanimously decided that the very next Sunday they would all meet the parson outside Christ Church in Union Street. There was Sam Tomms, Tommy Birch, George Mills and our dad. All four of them going to hear the parson preach for the sake of a free pint. None of them had ever been to a church service except when they got married or went to a funeral, gabbling words out of a prayer book like a lot of parrots.

As Sunday drew near, how they wished they hadn't promised to go and could back out, but none of them dared admit to one another that they were scared. The church was right at the bottom of the town about 8 to 10 minutes walk from Much Park Street. It was the smallest of the three spires of Coventry - St. Michael's, Holy Trinity and Christ Church and stood on the site of the old Greyfriars Monastery, to which the spire belonged. The church stood back from the road, just round the corner in Union Street, with iron railings and two sets of double gates in front and a few flowering shrubs in front of the railings. On either side of the little garden was a paved pathway leading up to four doors in the church. The middle ones were double doors leading into the church, the single doors on either side gave access to stone steps up to the galleries. The main doors led to a sort of vestibule, then there were green baize doors with little brass bolts top and bottom, which opened into the church. Over each door was an ornamental design in the stonework, giving the effect of a separate porch to each door. The middle doors were always open at 6pm for people to go in early if they wished. This allowed the altar to be on view from outside, also the brass lectern shaped like an eagle, where the lessons were read. Up the aisle was a red carpet and it all looked very inviting and cosy, but also rather frightening to four men who had never been inside a church for years.

When the service was in progress the front outside doors were left open but the green baize ones were shut, so latecomers could stand in the vestibule out of the weather and listen to whatever stage the service had reached. If they could hear the minister's voice chanting the prayers they stayed where they were, but if a hymn was being sung they went through the green baize doors and the verger, a man in a black gown like a cape with slits through which he put his arms, would come forward from somewhere at the back with a hymn book and prayer book and show them to a seat. This would usually be on the back row or at the side behind the huge pillars which supported the galleries, as all the best seats were taken up by the regular church-goers who paid 5/- a year pew rent, just for the privilege of sitting in the same seat every Sunday and having their name printed on a card and put in a slot at the front of the seat.

Sometimes during a sermon, if it was boring and no one else was sitting in the seat, they would slide along the seat away from their nameplate and sit behind one of the pillars and have forty winks. The pew tenant's always went through the middle doors, while the gallery doors were for the children and poorer people like our dad and his mates. The rented pews had pads on the seats and hassocks to kneel on when they prayed, but up in the gallery, if you wanted to pray, you either had to lean forward in your seat or kneel on the hard wooden floor.

The seats in the galleries were hard wooden ones, which went up in tiers on the steps. The Sunday school children always sat in the galleries in the mornings and afternoons, but never in the evenings, except at anniversary services. In the middle of the two galleries, at the back of the church, was the organ and choir, which was made up of men and women of all ages. It was what was called a low church, very much like non-conformist, but it was Church of England with the common prayer book, altar, lectern and pulpit. The ministers, vicar and curate wore surplices. There was no bowing by the clergy, not even at the altar, but there was definitely a class distinction amongst members of the congregation. The tradesmen of the town, butchers, bakers, builders, architects, solicitors, etc., were churchwardens and sidesmen. The works' manager and foreman of the factory where our dad worked were churchwardens at this church.

On the Sunday morning when they had promised to go to church the men went to the pub as soon as it was open and discussed, or rather cussed, going to church in the evening. By turning out time, they were full to overflowing with beer and courage, arguing what time they would have to be at the church and what they would wear.

Suddenly Tommy Birch, the shortest of the lot, even shorter than our dad, drew himself up to his full height of 5ft 2inches, feeling 10ft tall. 'What's all the fuss abaht? Anybody 'ud think we'd gorra preach the bloody sermon or sommat. All wem gorra do is sit on the back row of the gallery.'

'But 'ow do we get to the bloody gallery, if the parson ain't theer?' says our dad.

'Same way as yo bloody well gew up the gods at the Hippo,' says Tommy. 'An' don't forget to put a collar and tie on, no mufflers theer. Put a 1d in yor pocket an' all fer the collection, they come roun' wi' little red plush bags wi' wooden 'andles on 'em. We shall look bloody fools if we ain't gor any money ter put in the bag.'

'Ow do yo know all that?' says George Mills, the big man. 'I thought yo 'ad never bin ter church afore.'

'Oh,' says Tommy, as quick as lightening, 'my missus gus ter the mother's meeting sometimes. Her says as 'ow the parson preaches rattlin' good sermons. No noddin' off. Her sends the kids ter Sunday school on Sunday artnoons an' all, while her 'as five minutes.'

Our mam's face dropped a mile when she saw our dad staggering up the yard just after 2o'clock when the pub closed. She thought he'd never be fit to go to church, but as soon as he had eaten a big dinner he lay down on the sofa and slept like a baby until about 4pm. She made a strong cup of tea and woke him up. 'Come on, yove gorra get ready ter gew to that theer church,' she said.

When he woke up he started swearing, cursing the parson for making them promise they'd go to his bloody church, but mam said, 'That's enough swearing. Yo promised 'im yod gew.'

36

While he had been asleep she had been busy pressing his best suit, which he hadn't worn for months. It had been in 'uncle's' two or three times since he had last worn it and was all creased up. She was always in dread and fear when it was in pawn in case he wanted it all of a sudden and when she learned from the wife of one of the other men that they were all going to church on Sunday night, she rushed down to the pawnshop to 'pop' a blanket to get his suit out. She had sent us to Sunday school while he had his nap, but when she woke him up he was in such a bad mood she began to think he wouldn't go after all. But with all his cursing and swearing she knew he was afraid of his mates and wouldn't have the courage to face them all at the pub if he didn't turn up tonight. He got off the sofa and went into the little pantry place where we kept a bowl on a table with a jug of cold water underneath it. He poured out some water into the bowl. It was icy cold and although he grunted and grumbled, it woke him up.

Then came the performance of dressing him in his best suit. Putting on his collar and tie was the worst part. He always wore (when he did wear a collar) what he called a 'polo' collar, at least that is what we had to ask for when we went to buy one for him. He took size thirteen and a half. It had a sort of dickie arrangement at the front which tucked inside his waistcoat (westcut he called it), but it had to have a back stud as well as a front stud and these always had to be searched for in drawers and cupboards, such little things but so important, as the collar was no good without either of them and this held up all the other dressing operations. When the collar was fixed, then came the tie. If the collar was a new one, it sometimes had to be taken off again so that the tie could be put under the neck part of the collar, as it would be too stiff to get the tie straight while it was on the neck. I have known him take it off half a dozen times, cursing and swearing as he did so. The collar would get grubbier and grubbier until mam had to come to the rescue. He hated getting dressed up.

At last he was ready. It had taken him an hour and he had no time for any more tea, but my word he did look smart. What a transformation.

'He doesn't look the same man,' our mam said. When he put his bowler hat on, after she had brushed it, it being covered with dust, as he hadn't worn it for months, we couldn't take our eyes off him.

He banged out of the house and stood at the bottom of the court waiting for the others to come up. Old Sam was the first on and he said, 'My word, Ted lad, yo do look smart. Quite a good looker yo ar' when yom dressed up. Yo look as if yom goin' courtin' again. Bet the missus 'ad sommat ter say to yer. Must 'ave reminded 'er of bygone days.'

'Shut yor big gob, Sam. I've 'ad enough a'ready off 'er. I won' gew at all in a minute.'

Then up came the others all looking sheepish and furtively peering to left and right to make sure their missuses weren't watching them, or any of their other drinking pals from 'The Greyhound.' They all knew they would have to put up with sneers and gibes when next they went to the pub.

'Come on chaps, we're all 'ere now. Let's get this bloody business over and done wi',' said George Mills and off they went down the street, walking quickly as ever they could to get away from the neighbourhood. All this they were willing to put up with for the sake of that free pint.

When they arrived at the gate leading up to the church door, it was barely 6.15pm the time the parson said he would be there to meet them and show them where to sit. The bells were already ringing and the very sound of them and the sight of the people in their Sunday best walking towards the gate, made them want to turn round and run for it. But it was too late, the parson was already at the church door and as soon as he saw them approach the gate, he was down the path like a shot, for he knew exactly how they felt. He smiled at them and held out his hand to shake hands with them all, saying how pleased he was to see them. He shepherded them up the path to the side door, which led to the gallery steps. He was all in black, as he hadn't yet put on his 'preaching' gown, as old Sam called it.

Up the stone steps they all trooped, the parson leading the way. He proudly showed them to a row at the back, and it was a gallery indeed, just like the one at the Hippo, the only difference being these seats had backs to them, but you climbed up the steps just the same. Everybody looked up from down below as the noise of their heavy boots sounded like an army going over the bare boards. The parson gave them all hymn books and prayer books and left them as he had to get ready to take his place at the head of the choir stalls.

The bells were sounding one note now, which sounded like Come, Come, Come. The church was filling up quickly and some small boys came running up the steps of the gallery and sat in the front row making such a noise, giggling and nudging one another, as they looked round and saw a row of uncomfortable looking men at the back.

The organ started to play and the choir began to sing. The tune was a well known one, which the men knew and they soon forgot where they were and sang out loud and clear like they did at the pub when they had had one or two pints. The parson looked up and smiled to himself, so pleased that they all seemed to be enjoying themselves. After prayers there was another hymn, which he had chosen specially for them, 'Fight the good fight'. Then the parson went up the steps to the pulpit. He had decided not to preach a long sermon, but to come straight to the point. He didn't want to bore them the first time they came. He hoped they would come again, even if he had to bribe them with another pint. He felt sure if he persisted he would win at least one of them over. He was right. It was our dad he won over in the end. That Sunday evening service was, for him, a turning point in his life and ours.

At the end of the service Dad and his mates trooped down the steps of the gallery quickly, to try and beat the parson and all the posh people from down below, but he was already at the church door shaking hands with them again in front of all the other people. He said, 'I hope you have enjoyed the service. I will see you tomorrow night.' All the people round them heard him say that, but they didn't know where he would meet them 'Tomorrow night'. That was their secret.

12

They intended to go straight into the pub for a pint when they came out of church, but by now they felt so ashamed that not one of them had the courage. For the first time for many a long day they all went home. Much to the surprise of their families, especially the children, who couldn't make it out at all seeing their dad home so early.

They decided that they had better turn up on Monday night to receive their prize of a pint and face all their other mates in the bar. When they all trooped into the pub one after another, the atmosphere seemed strained and different somehow. Not one of them mentioned the free pint and the visit to the church, but all eyes were on the door waiting for the parson to come. Sure enough at exactly 8o'clock he came in, smiling all over his face and saying, 'Good evening, gentlemen.' He walked straight up to the counter and ordered five pints, but there was silence for a few seconds, then old Sam stood up, after a lot of nudging from his mates and said, 'Look 'ere parson, we don't rightly feel we oughter accept yor offer of a free pint 'cause we all enjoyed yor sermon so much. So we thought we would like to gie the money towards sommat for the black people out in them foreign parts. So if yo will accept that theer money from us chaps, we'll all feel better abaht it somehow.'

'Well that is very generous of you all,' said the parson, 'but we agreed that I should buy you all a pint and as I have ordered them now, I think the arrangement had better stand. I tell you what though. You all usually have two or three pints yourselves every night. How about putting the money for one pint in my missionary box and only having two instead of three on Friday night? I will bring the box with me the next time I come and you can put it in yourselves when you settle up for the week's beer.' So that was all agreed upon.

The parson was a real live wire though and realised he had still got to work hard to finish what he had begun by inviting them to the church. He knew that the men only lived a stone's throw away from the pub, so he decided that his next move was to visit their families in their own homes. The first family he visited was that of George Mills, in one of the courts nearby. George was a big, burly fellow, but his wife was a frail little woman with four children. She had to take in other people's washing although she had plenty of her own, but there was never enough money coming in for food, clothes, rent, etc. The oldest of the children was about seven or eight, a boy, and as frightened looking as his mother. The next one, also a boy, was about four years old, but not old enough to have much fear of anybody, as his

39

mother had always protected him and he hadn't started school yet. Most of the rows and fights had occurred after he had gone to bed and as he was used to a lot of noise he wasn't disturbed by the screaming and shouting when his father came home drunk. The older boy had not only heard all the screaming, but had witnessed the beating of his mother, as he was often still up when it happened and he was terrified of his father. He had decided in his mind that when he was a man he would somehow get his mother out of all this and have his revenge on his father.

The next child, a girl of three, was like her little brother, not old enough to take much notice of the noise, as she was also in bed when her father came home from the pub. The baby, also a girl, was about three months old. When she was born George cursed and swore at the fat old midwife when she came downstairs for some hot water and told him, 'It's another gel, George.' He went straight down to the pub, not asking how his wife was and did not return until after the landlord had shouted, 'Time gentlemen please.'

His wife, who lay trembling in her bed with the newborn baby, had entreated the midwife to stay the night, knowing too well what state George would be in when he came home. This particular night he had been hollering all over the bar about his wife having another 'bloody wench' and treating all his mates to the wetting of the baby's head. He was in such a drunken state at closing time that the landlord also feared for George's wife and helpless babe, and told the barman to fetch a policeman to follow him home. The policeman was standing at the bottom of the yard as George came reeling up.

'Hi, you just be quiet will yet and behave yourself. Your missus is ill in bed. If yer can't make less noise, I'll run yer in. My mate is at the bottom of the street and I've only got to blow me whistle and up he'll come.'

George heard what the policeman said and like all big bullies was a coward at heart, so he went up the yard and into his own door as quiet as a mouse, much to the surprise of his wife and the midwife.

'Good afternoon, Mrs Mills,' said the parson when she opened the door, after he had knocked several times. 'May I come in?'

Seeing the scared look on her face he said, 'Now don't worry. I see you are busy.' She had her sleeves rolled up as she was doing some washing and didn't ask him in as suggested, but kept him standing on the doorstep. She knew him all right.

He said, 'I only came to invite you to the mother's meeting on Monday afternoon. Mrs Charlton from the court just below is going and I thought it would be nice if you would come along with her as you know one another.'

She still had that frightened look on her face, so he said, 'Oh don't worry, your husband knows all about it. It was him who told me to ask you.'

Immediately her face brightened and she said, 'Well, yes I would like to come, but what about the children?'

'Oh, you can bring them along too. Well the three younger ones, the older boy goes to school doesn't he? You will be home by the time he comes out, or he can come along to you. Mrs Charlton is bringing along her little girl, the one who doesn't go to school and your children can play with her and all the other children in a little playroom at the back of the mission room, with someone in charge of them. There are plenty of toys for them to play with, which have been given to us. They will have a lovely time and I am sure will want to come again. You can keep the baby on your lap and you will have a nice rest away from the older children, a lovely cup of tea with a biscuit, all free and it doesn't matter if the baby makes a noise, there will be other babies there. The vicar's wife will take the meeting. She is a wonderful person and will see that everyone is happy.' All this the parson said, making it all sound so inviting to the poor woman, who had such a hard life and no enjoyment whatever.

That was how all the wives and mothers of the men who went to 'The Greyhound' started to go to the mothers' meeting every Monday afternoon. The children did enjoy the playroom, playing with toys they had never seen before, rocking horses, dolls, dolls' houses, etc., for the girls and train sets, building bricks and cowboy outfits for the boys. The mothers all enjoyed the meeting, free from the kids, with a free cuppa, biscuit and a natter with all the other women. The older children, including our Grace, used to go to their mothers straight from school, running all the way to get there as quickly as possible and the news spread round the courts like wild fire about the playroom with all those toys and the cups of tea for the mothers.

Soon, very soon, the mothers' meeting was full to overflowing and I can well remember seeing all the prams parked along the wall outside the mission room in Greyfriars Lane. In addition to the work of the mothers' meeting, the vicar's wife interested herself in the cause of temperance and started a movement, which she called 'catch my pal'. Visiting the mothers in their homes she saw for herself the terrible suffering and hardship their husbands inflicted on them and their families through drink. There were five or six pubs in every street and the drunkenness was indescribable. I can remember seeing men being thrown out into the street, rolling into the gutter, where they would lie too drunk to walk, until some of their pals, not quite so drunk, pulled them up and staggered home with them before the coppers came along and took them along to the police station in St. Mary's Street, where the cells were always full.

How wives must have dreaded hearing the unsteady footsteps coming up the yard on the cobblestones. If we had to pass the pubs going down the street and the door opened, the babble of voices would gain in volume with the amount of beer consumed and as it got near to closing time, it was as if it was coming from a loudspeaker the noise was so great.

The vicar's wife became so obsessed by the misery caused by all this drunkenness that she would go to the common lodging houses, or 'doss houses' as they were known, where men who had come into the town to find work could get a bed for the night. They had to live in appalling conditions. The 'doss houses' were generally derelict foundries and warehouses, up courts behind old houses, where the men cooked their own breakfasts in their own utensils over a fire in the rusty ranges, which had been left behind. They used to try and hide their frying pans and other utensils, but often when they came in from work (if they had any), their 'grub' and other things had been used or pinched altogether. They would then go out and get drunk at the nearest pub with no food in their bellies and come back ready for a fight. They would snatch other men's frying pans off the fire and a riot would soon start, with all of them fighting one another. There would be Irish, Scots, Welsh, all sorts. If it got too bad the proprietor would send for a copper to eject the worst offenders.

It was to this kind of place that the vicar's wife used to go, on her own, to try and get the men to join the temperance campaign. Of course, there were a lot of the men who would take advantage of her and go to the vicarage to plead poverty, promising faithfully to 'go straight' just to get food and clothing and money for decent lodgings. She also found employment for some of them to try and keep them sober. This would last a few weeks in most cases, as the temptation would be so great they would drift back to their old habits.

Their environment, of course, was against them. It was practically impossible to lead a decent life and only about two out of about thirty kept straight. She eventually gave her life for the 'catch my pal' movement. One night in the depth of winter when she was ill with influenza, she got up out of her bed to rescue some poor destitute and caught pneumonia from which she died. All the 'drop outs' cried genuine tears, they all knew they had lost a true friend who really cared for their welfare and had given her life for them.

13

The parson continued to visit the men in the bar at 'The Greyhound' and was on very good terms with them and they in turn looked upon him with great respect. But he hadn't been able to persuade them to pay another visit to his church, not even with the promise of a free pint. They all kept backing out. He also kept in touch with their wives through the mothers' meeting, but now he thought he must interest the children and complete the family circle. He invited them all to come to the Sunday school and the 'Band of Hope', which was a temperance meeting for children, held every Tuesday evening at the mission room in Greyfriars Lane. It was the same place where the mothers' meetings were held, so the children knew where it was.

The majority of the children came from the surrounding district, slums and courts like ours, only worse if that was possible. There were as many as seven and eight children in one house, with half a dozen closets to a court of twenty to thirty houses, all infested with fleas and bugs. The children would run round the communal water tap in the centre of the yards in rags, with no boots on their feet and 'pieces' in their fists for a meal, with lard or dripping on the bread, never butter.

At the bottom of the mission room entry was a little shop where sometimes we used to spend a farthing of the halfpenny we had been given for the collection. The sweets were usually jap nuggets, screwed up in a piece of newspaper. Once inside the mission room the teacher could handle all of us even the tough nuts from the neighbouring courts, but as we waited outside in the yard for opening time, the boys behaved like wild animals, punching one another and rolling on the ground. The caretaker who lived in a house nearby was always threatening to report them to the teacher, but it happened every week and we were always glad to get inside.

We all took part in the meeting, singing and reciting. Grace and I used to sing together. The teacher organised concerts, which were a huge success, because we all loved her so much and she got such good results. The parents were invited and everybody got excited. We used to do sketches and musical items, popular tunes of the day such as *Poor Old Joe* and *I don't want to play in your yard*. We did *The Emperor Napoleon had a Feather in his Cap* with all the actions and many others. One little musical sketch I remember was *Caller Herrin'* and we were all dressed as fisher girls with a basket on our arms with real herrings in it. We had bare feet and a little shawl round our shoulders. It was a huge success and we could always be sure of an encore whenever we did it. *Land of Hope and Glory* was another success, with one of the girls playing Britannia. She would be seated high up in the centre of the stage with her long fair hair all draped around her shoulders, complete with the regalia of Britannia. The audience must have thought she looked wonderful for when the curtain went up there would be a long applause. Everybody seemed more patriotic in those days prior to the 1914-18 war.

14

We were too young to know just what mam had on her mind, but we could see that she was worried over something and knew she was determined to get us out of that court and that street somehow. She had heard that there was a new estate about to be built in the fields around London Road, at the back of the old Charterhouse, the medieval building founded by King Richard II for the Carthusian monks nearly 600 years ago. It stood in its own grounds surrounded by a high wall.

Mam wasn't quite sure how to go about it. She knew the rent would be higher, as it would be a new house straight on to the pavement, not up a court like ours. She had nobody to turn to for help. Our dad was not in agreement (they were always quarrelling about it), nor was our gran. They had lived in the court all their lives and didn't want to go far away from 'The Greyhound'. Mam didn't want to keep going to the pawnshop as the articles pawned had to be redeemed somehow. This was a constant worry to mam and thousands like her. Old Samuels charged a halfpenny interest a month and if at the end of twelve months the articles were not redeemed, they were lost forever and he sold them for much more than he had paid on them.

One afternoon mam suddenly made up her mind to go and see the builder. It took quite a lot of courage, but mam was a fighter, nothing daunted her proud spirit. She had much perseverance. She dressed herself up in her best clothes and looked quite smart. She was quite pretty with her dark hair and china blue eyes. She had on a black hat trimmed with feathers and a tight-fitted jacket and a skirt with three or four frills at the bottom, edged with black satin baby ribbon. The jacket and skirt she had bought from a second-hand clothes shop and it had been altered to fit her. It was very full, with yards of material in it. The fullness of the skirt was gathered together at the back in a sort of bunch held with a skirt clasp, which opened and shut with a kind of spring. The skirt was very long and the clip kept it up off the ground out of the dirt and also made it easier to walk, but it was sometimes necessary to hold it up with one hand when going up steps. Crinolines had only just gone out of fashion and this was a new idea. Round the waist she wore a belt made of metal medallions all joined together, with two large clasps at the front to fasten it.

When she arrived at the building site, where the builder had his office, mam was overcome with nervousness and walked about for a few minutes afraid to go in, then she turned round and boldly knocked on the door. A gruff voice said, 'Come in.' She entered timidly and was confronted by a rough looking man with a cloth cap on his head, who didn't look at all like the builder she had imagined.

'Good afternoon,' he said, without looking up.

'Good afternoon,' said mam in a quiet voice.

'And what can I do for you?' he said, suddenly turning his head and looking her up and down.

'Are you Mr Forester, the builder,' she asked in a tremulous voice.

'Yes I am,' he said.

'Well I came to see if I could have my name put down for one of your houses when they are finished,' said mam.

Still staring at her, he asked abruptly, 'Can you pay the rent. It will be 5/9d a week.'

'Yes, I think so,' said mam.

'You think so. You have got to be sure. Where do you live now?'

Mam went very red and with downcast eyes told him our address. He looked her up and down again and said in his gruff voice, 'You've got pluck woman. The houses will be sold for £180 when they are finished and if any are sold for investment, I will put your name forward as a tenant, but the landlord will of course require a week's rent in advance. I will let you know when they are ready. Good afternoon.'

Poor mam, this was a blow. How on earth was she going to be able to pay 5/9d and 3/6d all in one week. She didn't understand what he meant by investment. Existence was the only word she understood. At last, she succeeded in overcoming overwhelming obstacles and we did move into our new house and that was the beginning of our changed world, but that is another story.

Left:
Edwin & Fanny Raby

Below:
Florence & Fred Jones Wedding.
1926.

Left:
Beatrice Callow, Ted Raby,
Philip Callow
& Fanny Raby. c.1926

Bottom Left:
Florence Raby.

Bottom Right:
Beatrice & John.
Vecqueray Street
Coventry
c. 1930

Above:
Beatrice, Herbert,
Philip & John.
Barford, Warwick
1930's

Right:
Beatrice Callow.
Rhyl 1930

Left:
Beatrice at Bassett Road
Coventry
September 1948.

Bottom Left:
Beatrice Callow as a teenager.

Bottom Right:
Hubert & Beatrice Callow.
Isle of Man. 1936.

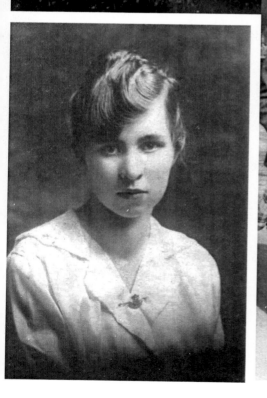

Issues Raised in Hurdy Gurdy Days

City and Housing

At the beginning of the nineteenth century Coventry was still fundamentally a medieval city. Development had taken place throughout the century, mainly the infilling of space behind existing housing, causing severe overcrowding. Courts and back-to-back housing were the result, becoming a feature of the city. Expansion had taken place outside the old walled area of the city along arterial roads such as Gosford Street and Spon Street. Hillfields was the first district to be developed from 1828, specifically as a ribbon weaving quarter. Chapelfields grew as an extension to the Spon Street watch-making district, followed by Earlsdon.

In 1842 the first boundary extension increased the area of the city to 1,486 acres. Other extensions followed in 1890 and 1899 giving an area of 4,147 acres. It was the freeing of the Michaelmas and Lammas lands in 1860 and 1875, which eventually allowed the city to expand. The Freemen of Coventry had a right to graze animals on these lands, which they gave up in exchange for other areas of land, which yielded an income. The developments on the periphery, such as Earlsdon were swallowed up in these extensions. The need to expand reflects the tremendous growth of the city at that time. Workers from far and near were attracted by the prospect of employment in the many small factories which were emerging. Sewing machines, bicycles and the burgeoning motor industry were taking over prominence, as first the ribbon weaving and then the watch-making industries declined.

The period covered by Beatrice Callow's *Hurdy Gurdy Days* runs from the end of the nineteenth century and into the early twentieth century, at a time of rapid change and increasing population, which put great strain upon the resources of the city. In 1875 the population stood at 39,446, by 1905 it had increased to 75,134. One man who knew at first hand what these figures meant was the Medical Officer of Health (MOH) E. Hugh Snell M.D. His Annual Health Reports graphically illustrate the problems encountered through overcrowding and the insanitary conditions in which so many people lived.

The Housing of the Working Class Act of 1890 gave the Local Authorites the power to demolish unfit houses if they were insanitary, if they were an obstruction, or for street widening schemes. Despite the noble sentiments of the act, it was impossible to implement its provisions over a short period of time. The majority of the working class housing within the city would have been condemned on insanitary grounds alone, but in fact the bulk of those that were removed were cleared for road widening purposes. The procedure for condemning a house as unfit for human habitation was a long drawn out process. First of all a notice of improvement was issued against the owner, then a period of time elapsed for work to be carried out. Sometimes this could be years. Often improvements made were inadequate anyway, putting off the day when the property would eventually be condemned. Many such properties were owned by speculative landlords, whose only interest was the weekly rent. As Beatrice Callow's mother found when she approached the rent collector for improvements to be carried out, the answer was a firm 'NO.' Landlords relied on the fact that tenants would not inform the authorities or make trouble, for fear of being evicted.

The efficiency of the process is illustrated in this table covering the ten years from 1891-1900.

Table 1

Year	Condemned by MOH	Improved in consequence	Closed	Back-to-backs made through Ventilated
1891	62	9	6	18
1892	42	10	29	
1893	36	8	33	10
1894	6	5	1	4
1895	15	5	1	6
1896	9		4	
1897	2		2	
1898	4	2		
1899	31	12	12	6
1900	75	30	5	6
	283	80	93	50

Medical Officer of Health Report 1900

It is evident from this table that the system was not working, it was being abused and the law was colluding with the owners to perpetuate the appalling standard of living people were made to endure. In 1900 matters did begin to improve and enforcement became more strict, as the final figures imply; even so, only five houses were actually closed. The MOH believed that harsher measures should be taken against recalcitrant landlords. Unfortunately, only magistrates had the power to force closure, not the sanitary authority. One of the worst areas around Leicester Street, on the north side of the city centre, was demolished in 1900 to widen the road, rather than as a consequence of the bad housing.

Overcrowding was another source of concern to the MOH. Official figures for the average number of persons occupying each belie the cramped conditions in which many lived.

1891 = 4.5; 1897 = 4.9; 1898 = 4.8; 1899 = 4.7; 1900 = 4.7.
Medical Officer of Health Report 1900.

However, there were numerous families like that of Nellie Brookes in *Hurdy Gurdy Days*, with eleven children and two adults in a court dwelling of a single room downstairs, one first floor bedroom and an attic room. The MOH believed landlords should be held responsible for overcrowding, although what landlords could do when tenants were unable or unwilling to pay more rent for a larger property is a debatable point. The larger the family the more their resources would be stretched, for their outlay on food would be a larger proportion of their income than those with less mouths to feed. As the children grew older and contributed their wages to the family income the rental of a larger house might be possible, but no doubt if it came to a choice of better food or additional space, food would be more desirable.

Efforts were being made to improve and increase the housing stock immediately outside the old city wall. The majority of this development was carried out by private enterprise, but the Corporation also initiated schemes to provide reasonably priced, rented accommodation in the first decade of the twentieth century. This chart shows how much construction had taken place at the end of the nineteenth century.

Table 2.

Wards	Occupied houses 1891	Vacant houses 1891	Vacant houses 1900	Built since 1891	Demolished since 1891	Population census 1897
Gosford St	2,876	32	40	762	65	15,247
Bishop St	2,742	24	46	985	16	1 4,820
Earl St	2,182	67	51	556	16	12,389
Whitefriars	1,935	117	36	83	41	9,477
Spon St	1,735	44	56	321	68	9,058
North East			63	113*	9*	
	11,470	284	292	2,820	215	60,991

* 1900 only

Medical Officer of Health Report 1900

The north east of the city, including Foleshill and part of Stoke, had been added with the 1899 boundary extension leading to inadequate figures for this period. During the decade covered, nearly 1,000 houses were built in the Bishop Street ward alone. This was due to the creation of new roads in the north of the city. The Bishop Street ward covered an area from Middleborough Road in Radford, across Foleshill Road, Stoney Stanton Road and into Red Lane and part of Hillfields, including the many streets in between. In that same period only sixteen houses were demolished, yet the inner city area of this ward held some of the worst slum dwellings.

At the beginning of the twentieth century many more houses were being improved rather than condemned. There was still some back-to-back housing in 1902, but many had been made through ventilated by this time. Through

47

ventilation usually required the adjustment of internal walls to make one dwelling from two back-to-backs. Within the court system of Coventry, where homes had been built around the edge of an existing courtyard, without another dwelling attached to the back, extra ventilation was required. Sometimes the houses fronting the street were removed to open up the court and allow a freer flow of air. This solution was a particular feature of the way Birmingham dealt with the problem. The MOH proved that the death rate was much higher in back-to-backs, as the air in courts became foetid due to standing water and accumulated rubbish. Frequently tenants remained in occupation during the alterations and repairs to the property, for they had nowhere else to go.

On 26th February 1912 the City Engineer and Surveyor, J.E. Swindlehurst, produced a report on the expansion of Coventry in the previous twelve years. Following the boundary extention of 1899, 1,466 acres were made available for building. Only by expanding could the congestion of the city centre be relieved. Between 1st January 1900 and 31st January 1911 forty-nine 'estates' were laid out. An estate in Swindlehurst's terms would mean just a street or two, a small parcel of land developed by a builder. Those forty-nine estates numbered 141 streets, with a total length of 17.85 miles. Houses numbering 6,762 or 64.5% of the total, had been or were in the process of being erected, leaving another 3,724 or 35.5% to be built. Bylaws governed the width of the road, the area at the rear of the building and the height of the rooms, as well as the number of properties that could be erected within a given area. All properties had to be connected to mains drainage. It cost approximately £240 to purchase an average house on one of these estates.

The most congested streets had 61 dwellings per gross acre, 71 per net acre. An example given by Swindlehurst of a less congested estate was that of Albany Road, Earlsdon. The width of the road was 40ft, with just 29.7 houses per net acre. He obviously considered roads too wide, labelling them 'wastes of macadam,' but he was constrained by regulations from making them any narrower. He was also of the opinion that too many regulations discouraged builders from buying land for development, but they were there to prevent a situation arising, which had blighted the city centre for so long. The planners were looking to the future and a better life for working class families, as well as foreseeing a city where the motor car would reign supreme.

In an effort to accommodate the poorer workers, who could not afford the rent of a new house on an estate, tenements were built. One instance cited by Swindlehurst was of 22 tenements erected in Short Street by the Corporation, which consisted of a living room, one bedroom and a scullery bathroom. Even these properties commanded a rental of 4s 3d per week, still beyond the purse of many.

In 1902 there were 15,743 tenements within the city, of which 8,916 had less than five rooms. Most consisted of one living room and one bedroom, 375 of these were inhabited by four or more persons. Of the tenements with three rooms, one living room, and two bedrooms, some 90 contained between eight and eleven persons. The authorities received anonymous letters informing them of gross overcrowding, but during that year only six cases were brought to court. A consequence of this might be the splitting up of the family and removal to the workhouse, an action dreaded by all. In 1904, 26 cases of overcrowding were dealt with and 23 cases in 1905.

Artisans dwellings, of two and three bedrooms, were the most in demand. Only 15.5% of the whole housing stock on the estates built in the twelve years to December 1911 had baths, but all had a separate W.C. and were provided with a dustbin. Rents were higher than those of city centre courts and tenements as one would expect, but as Mrs Charlton decided, within their means if they were careful. This table from Swindlehurst's report shows the proportion of houses in each rental class. Weekly rentals included rates.

Table 3.

	5/3--5/11	6/-6/11	7/-7/11	8/-8/11	over 10/-
Approx number of houses.	578	3,398	928	1,248	610
% of total houses erected.	8.5	50.2	13.8	18.5	9.0

12 years to December 1911.
J.E. Swindlehurst.

Although Mrs Charlton's rent in the new property was 5s 9d, at the lowest scale of this table, it was a considerable step up from the Much Park Street dwelling.

New properties were being built all the time, but these too were usually beyond the means of those most in need of them. Even the Corporation housing development in Narrow Lane, intended for working class tenants, charged a rental of 5s 6d per week. Empty property existed within the city too, see Table 2. In 1900, 292 houses stood empty. Rents of these houses were as follows:

£20 and upwards per year	99
5s 6d -7s 6d per week	63
2s 6d - 5s per week	130
	292

Medical Officer of Health Report 1900.

The largest number was in the lowest category of rentable property, so why were they not snapped up? Presumably they were either no better than those they already occupied, or they were still beyond the means of many who could not afford even a slight increase in rent. In 1904 there were 547 empty houses, 261 more than in 1903, of those 207 were in the 2s 6d bracket, but significantly only one under 2s 6d.

The Charltons paid a rent of 3s 6d for their home in a Much Park Street court, certainly not on the lowest level of accommodation, yet this house should have been condemned. It had no water, no drainage, crumbling walls and peeling paint. Women like Mrs Charlton and Mrs Trapp worked hard to keep their inferior homes in some sort of order. It was a source of pride to them to make the best of a bad job and prove to their neighbours that they might be poor, but they were clean. All water had to be carried from the communal tap and heated on the range. This alone required a considerable effort. The washing involved several changes of water, pounding the clothes with a dolly, carrying the wet clothes to the mangle in the yard, back for the rinsing and re-mangling. On fine days the whole process would be carried out in the yard, but on wet days it would have been done indoors and only the mangling done outside. Even pegging out the inadequately wrung articles on the line required more effort and again the weather was a deciding factor and it might have to be hung inside. No wonder women like Mrs Brookes just gave up under the strain of trying to manage. Beatrice Callow complained of the chores she and her sister had to perform at the behest of their mother, but this early training probably helped them to understand the hardship endured by their mother. It is hard to understand why Mrs Brookes did not get her children to help carry water and perform cleaning jobs. Some of her children must have been capable of doing so, but she had been so beaten down by poverty and hardship that she no longer had the inclination to make that effort.

Common Lodging Houses
For those who came to Coventry for work, but could not afford to rent accommodation, there were common lodging houses, where a bed could be obtained at little cost. Rules and regulations governed the running of these houses, under the supervision of the sanitary authority. These premises required a licence and the number of lodgers prescribed, although this was often flouted. In 1898 the law required that each lodger should have a given space per person. In comparison with other institutions it fared badly.

Table 4.
    250 cu ft per person in lodging houses.
    300 cu ft per person in the workhouse.
    600 cu ft per person in a military barracks.
    800 cu ft per person in a prison cell.
    1,200 cu ft per person in hospital.
Medical Officer of Health Report 1898.

Later lodging house space was increased to 400 cu ft per person. In 1898 only two came up to standard in Coventry. During that year the older houses were brought up to standard, so that all six complied with the law. They accommodated a total of 147 lodgers. A warden had to reside at the lodging house and keep a daily record of inmates. By 1901 there were twelve common lodging houses on the register, although that year a case of smallpox began in one of these houses. This must have galvanised the authorities into greater vigilance, as there were only five houses by 1903.

Houses were also let in lodgings, under supervision, but did not require a resident keeper. The number of these remained fairly static. In 1898 there were twelve such properties, but by 1903 that number had dropped to ten. The common lodging houses seemed to be where trouble started, as mentioned by Beatrice Callow. These were frequented by the more casual workers, looking for a bed overnight. Fights would start over petty pilfering and were exacerbated by the high incidence of drunkenness in such places.

Those who could not even afford the dubious comforts of a common lodging house would resort to the workhouse, where a bed was provided for itinerant travellers, provided they took a bath first. A meeting of the Coventry Board of Guardians was reported in the *Coventry Herald* of 17th February 1905, stating that tramps were taking advantage of the provision of beds at the workhouse on a Saturday night and moving on during Sunday. They proposed that the tramps should be detained on the Sunday and not released until the Monday, to discourage them from making use of the service. This was adopted, although some would have liked to detain them from Friday to Monday, if space had allowed.

Drunkenness

Drunkenness caused great hardship and misery, in a society such as that described by Beatrice Callow. It affected the lives of so many of her contemporaries from their earliest years. In her story it is the men of the family who wasted their earnings in the pub, leaving their families short of cash for the necessities of life. However, life could be even worse if the wife also drank and neglected her children. In such cases those children might end up being farmed out to relatives, bringing themselves up or being put into the workhouse. Only Beatrice Callow's grandmother comes in for criticism on this score, the other women in her story seem to be making the best of their situation.

In the *Coventry Herald* of 17th February 1905 there was a report of a meeting of the Stoke Debating Society on the subject of 'Drunkenness and Poverty in Stoke'. Dr. Richardson Rice put forward the case that drunkenness caused poverty, as too much of the income of the poor was spent on drink. Sobriety, he claimed, would produce more and better workers. He blamed 15-20% of lunacy on the effects of alcohol. He pressed for the reduction of licensing hours as a solution. He also believed children should be educated about the dangers of alcohol. In reply, a Mr Wormall counteracted the arguments of Dr Richardson Rice by stating that it was not drink that caused poverty, but low wages. He asserted that the better off consumed two and a half times more alcohol than the poor, but no one condemned them for the practice.

Why did the men spend so much of their earnings upon drink when they could clearly see that it deprived their families of so much? Beatrice Callow's explanation is centred on the cheerlessness of the home, but that is too simple. Mrs Charlton made her home as cosy as possible; it was always warm, for the range was alight throughout the day, winter or summer. It was cramped, admittedly, but they were not used to having space. They only had two children and three adults in the house, very different from the Brookes' household. Mr and Mrs Charlton seemed a companionable couple, not at each other's throats all the time. So why did he retreat to the pub every night and spend what little money he had on drink?

The sort of spit and sawdust pub that the men frequented was surely not much more comfortable than the homes they had left. It was the companionship of their peers that was the attraction. They could talk and boast to their friends, it was an ego boost. These men had no status except amongst their own kind. They did menial jobs all day, labouring or taking orders from those in charge, for pitiable wages. It was only when they came together in the evening that they could be free from restraint. They could not take their friends home, for none of their houses would accommodate a gathering, so it was the pub, which became their meeting place. Buying a drink was a way of paying for your space and one drink led to another. Alternatively you could argue that what these men wanted was oblivion, as a means of coping with their poverty.

The Greyhound pub, like all pubs had its regular clientele, who had their beer on the slate throughout the week and paid their dues when they received their wages on a Friday night. Many of these pubs had an entrance from one of the courts as well as from the street. The MOH campaigned to have these back entrances closed, believing it to be a temptation to the occupants. I am sure, however, that a short walk to the front entrance would have deterred no one.

It is easy to condemn these men for drinking, especially those who turned violent and attacked their wives and children, or who picked fights with others. Mrs Graves was one such woman who suffered at the hands of a drunken husband. Repeatedly beaten, she stoically endured the wrath of her husband to protect her children. Once they had died, she gave up and retreated to the workhouse to die. She could have escaped to the workhouse with her children and maybe they would have been fed and looked after away from her brutal husband. Domestic violence had a taboo about it, neighbours were reluctant to get involved, but women did take their husbands to court and prosecute them for violence. Police court reports in the *Coventry Herald* frequently mention cases of women suing for a separation order from violent husbands. On 12th January 1900, June Cosford, 13court 33house St. John's Street, applied for a separation order on the grounds of persistent cruelty and desertion. Her husband had threatened her with a knife. One of her daughters gave evidence in her favour and she was granted her separation and custody of the children. Mr Cosford was ordered to pay 10s per week maintenance. The same paper featured the case of the wife of Henry Chittem, who used the Married Women's Act to obtain a separation from her husband on the grounds of assault and demanding money from her. A separation was granted and as she could support herself, no maintenance was levied. In this case there were no children. In another case reported at the same time, brought by the NSPCC against one Henry Sayers, 5court 10house Chauntry Place, for neglecting his wife and children, by not giving them any money. The case was settled when he agreed to pay housekeeping. Numerous cases appeared like this every week.

The majority of cases brought before the courts involved alcohol in some way - men and women becoming drunk and disorderly, getting into fights and frequently assaulting police officers when they tried to make an arrest. Usually the fines and costs levied depended on the severity of the charge. A fine had the alternative of hard labour. Charles Orton of Chauntry Place, found drunk in charge of a horse and cab in Well Street on 30th December 1899, was fined £1 plus costs or fourteen days imprisonment.

The courts were the province of men, who formed the judiciary and the juries. Although the evidence of the cases cited illustrate that women were treated with a consirerable amount of sympathy in the police courts, it was not always the case at higher courts. At the County Sessions reported on 27th January 1905 in the Coventry Herald, one Thomas Bacon Jones, a carpenter, of 1 Marian Terrace, Little Heath, Foleshill, was accused of persistant cruelty to his wife. She was requesting a separation and maintenance order. Her husband counter claimed that it was she who was a drinker and caused the trouble. When she was asked how much she drank she stated that she had a half-pint of beer with her lunch, dinner and supper. Her husband had a key to the barrel and doled it out, so she could not have more. This caused great mirth amongst the occupants of the court. She admitted to being drunk on one occasion and this condemned her in the eyes of the court. The judge dismissed the case and refused her a separation order. The double standards of this case are appalling. Presumably the husband was in the habit of drinking or he would not have provided himself with a barrel of beer, but at no time was he asked how much he consumed. He had beaten her up on many occasions, but that was dismissed as being irrelevant and she was blamed for this situation.

The police on the beat were more sympathetic to the plight of wives terrorised by their husbands. On the night that George Mills' wife produced a baby daughter, much to his disgust, it was the landlord of 'The Greyhound' who informed the beat policeman that there might be trouble in the court. The policeman then waited for George to come staggering into the yard on his way home to his wife, in a foul mood and ready for an argument or fight. Effectively the policeman defused the situation with a threat of a night in the cells.

Neighbours
The mother was of vital importance to the family of the poor. She it was who had to manage on a very limited budget. Beatrice Callow presents her mother as a good manager and a hard worker, but she could not manage on the money given to her

by her husband. She always put away the rent money without fail, she kept the house as clean and tidy as the circumstances allowed and she kept the family fed as nutritiously as she could. However, it was obvious that she frequently had to pawn possessions to make ends meet. She did part-time jobs to make a little extra money, but it was never enough, hence the arrears on the doctor's book and the desperate measures when her daughter Grace was taken ill.

Women were ground down by their poverty. Men had their pocket money - that percentage of their wages that they kept back for their own personal use, to spend on drink, cigarettes or gambling. Beatrice Callow does not say how much her father earned, or what he gave her mother in housekeeping, she probably did not know, for most women never knew what their husbands earned. The men would probably have been pressed for a higher proportion if they had known. The more children a woman had in these circumstances the harder it was for her to manage. Repeated pregnancy took its toll physically upon a woman's health, well illustrated in the case of Mrs Brookes. Eleven children surviving, possibly others miscarried or died through illness. This unfortunate woman, who had once been pretty, according to Mrs Charlton, but now sadly faded prematurely, had done a remarkable job in raising eleven children on very little. She may have appeared frail and crushed by poverty, but still had spirit enough to challenge Mrs Charlton to a fight when the cleanliness of her house and children were in question. Not all the spirit had been driven out of her; it only needed the right trigger to bring it to the fore.

Women helped each other in the network of courts. In the Charlton's court Mrs Trapp was the older woman, with a wealth of experience and a heart of gold whom everyone called upon in a crisis. She was a woman past childbearing age with grown up children who lived at home and contributed to the household budget and a husband in the army with a regular wage. She helped out during illness and laid out the dead. When Grace was taken ill with diphtheria, it was Mrs Trapp who was there to help. Mrs Charlton did not seek help from her own family who lived nearby, but asked for and received immediate help from Mrs Trapp. Where was her husband, was he still at work or in the pub? No one seems to have sought him or expected any help from him or his mother.

The two elderly neighbours in the court, Mrs Greasley and Mrs Smithers, near the end of their lives had to manage as best they could. Mrs Greasley, crippled with arthritis and bedridden for most of the time was helped by the generosity of her neighbours. She would not seek charity for assistance in her desperate situation, but lived on only 5s per week. Without money to buy fuel she had no fire, which must have made her arthritis much worse. Perhaps she refused to apply for outdoor parish relief, because she thought that the officers would consider it cheaper to accommodate her within the workhouse system and that was something she dreaded. Her rent would have taken at least half her income, leaving only 2s 6d or less for everything else, no wonder she had so little. What was the source of her income? Beatrice Callow says she received 5s pension per week, but old age pensions did not come into effect until 1908 and then only to those over seventy, provided that they had led an honest and industrious life in the previous ten years. Was it parish relief after all? If so her neighbours would certainly have been aware of the fact. She only entered the workhouse after a stroke, which deprived her of speech and movement.

Mrs Smithers too was a pathetic old lady living in poverty, despite having a working son living with her. She had only one leg and cateracts had caused blindness. Those cateracts, which could so easily be removed today, had to be endured. Both Mrs Greasley and Beatrice Callow's gran were completely deaf, possibly due to middle ear infection in early life. Mrs Smithers had a son of thirty, so she was unlikely to be much older than sixty years, however, her description suggests an ancient woman. Poverty truly aged people.

In my research I was able to find these two old ladies and discovered the circumstances of their deaths. I found out that their names were Mary Ann Glaze (Mrs Greasley) and Elizabeth Smith (Mrs Smithers). They were both entered in the voters list for 1905 at 11house and 13house 33court Much Park Street respectively. They both died in the workhouse, but much later than that suggested by Beatrice Callow. Mary Ann Glaze died aged 80, on 15th March 1915 and Elizabeth Smith died aged 87, on 16th March 1920. It seems likely that Beatrice Callow's family continued to visit the neighbours in their old court for many years after they moved away. This explains the anomalies of the pension, as it was much later than that put forward in the narrative.

Health

Illness was ever present in the overcrowded conditions in which the poor lived in Coventry, as it was in any other city. The death rate was frequently higher than the national average during our period. With poor drainage, bad housing, rubbish accumulating in courts and streets, the potential was there for a flare up of disease. The undernourished and sickly residents were more vulnerable and none more so than children. Infectious diseases were classed as 'zymotic' diseases, including smallpox, scarlet fever, diphtheria, typhoid fever, measles, whooping cough and diarrhoea. By far the greatest killer was diarrhoea. In 1897 it accounted for 69% of all zymotic deaths, 74 of the 80 deaths were children under the age of 5 years. The MOH reports always included an overall picture of the weather conditions for that year. Diarrhoea was especially prevalent during hot, dry summers. This was stated as one of the chief causes, probably because the water supply was less efficient at that time or water was left standing in open containers, after collection from the pump, leaving it open to contamination. Other reasons included overcrowding, density of buildings, too many courts, poor ventilation (there were still 3,046 back-to-back houses in 1897), dirtiness of dwellings, sewer and cess pool emanations and rubbish. Drainage had been improved by the end of the nineteenth century, but there were still some untrapped street gullies. Also there was still no systematic collection of rubbish, leaving domestic rubbish accumulating, which attracted vermin. During the summer months there were not so many fires on which to burn rubbish, especially with the increased use of gas stoves. The following year 1898, the number of deaths from diarrhoea increased to 131 of which 63 were infants. From this high point, deaths due to this cause lessened each year.

Bottle fed infants were very susceptible to diarrhoea, picking up infection from the teats and bottles, which had not been sterilized. Beatrice Callow's father had survived against all the odds when his mother frequently left him to fend for himself as a toddler, with only a bottle tied to his clothes. His siblings were not so lucky and succumbed to disease before he was born. His widowed mother had to work to keep a roof over their heads, unable to afford any kind of child-care, she must have considered that there was no alternative. His stunted growth was probably the result of this neglect and poor feeding. All manner of dirt and germs could be picked up while a child played in the yard. Food could be contaminated if it was stored in dirty, damp and poorly ventilated conditions. Flies might alight on uncovered food and spread disease. Personal hygiene was not widely understood, leading to contamination of shared toilets, which passed to food and was then consumed.

Greater public awareness of the dangers to infants came about through better education. The appointment of a female health visitor temporarily in 1901 did much to spread the message of better practice in feeding infants, where breast-feeding was impossible. Although the experiment was deemed a great success, a full-time female health visitor was not appointed until 1905. Her job included visits in connection with infectious and other diseases, in regard to cleanliness, calls on new mothers under the Midwives' Act and giving advice on care and hygiene. As if that was not enough for one individual, her job also included inspecting workshops where women were employed and visiting shops under the Shop Hours Act 1892 and Shop Assistants' Act 1899 to check that they were abiding by the law.

Some infectious diseases had to be notified to the MOH, including smallpox, scarlet fever, diphtheria and typhoid fever. Measles was no longer a notifiable disease after 1896, despite the fact that there were more deaths from measles in 1897 than the four notifiable diseases put together. The MOH thought it was a retrograde step. Whooping cough and diarrhoea were not notifiable either, but they too were responsible for a substantial number of deaths, especially diarrhoea as we have seen.

Diphtheria was a very serious disease, with a case mortality greater than any of the other notifiable zymotic diseases during this period.

Table 5

Year	Notified	Died	Case mortality %
1897	14	4	28.5
1898	20	5	25.0
1899	38	5	13.1
1900	66	22	33.3
1901	139	31	22.3
1902	136	30	22.1
1903	127	34	26.7
1904	78	11	14.1
1905	67	13	19.4

Medical Officer of Health Report 1905

The years 1901-3 show a very high incidence of the disease. The MOH recommended that cases should be isolated, but this was obviously not common practice. In 1897, of the 14 cases notified only one was isolated in hospital. Serum treatment was the only means at the disposal of the doctors to combat the symptoms of the disease. From 1902 a free supply of anti-diphtheria serum was available to the medical profession, but was not always taken advantage of. It gave a greater chance of recovery to patients if used early. The MOH remarked in 1903 that many local authorities had placed the facilities for obtaining assistance in the bacteriological examination of throat swabs, but that Coventry was lax in providing such services. In his words, 'Your city is the only area in this country where this is not done, both in relation to this and other diseases.' *(E.Hugh Snell, MOH Report 1903, p81).*

Grace Charlton obviously did receive this serum treatment, but her mother had to pay dearly for it. No doubt many others had to pawn items to raise the necessary cash for such treatments. The doctor seemed completely indifferent to the sufferings of the poor. Many believed that the poor brought such afflictions upon themselves, by their fecklessness, drinking and squalid conditions. However, they made no allowances for those who were trying their best in difficult circumstances to live on a very limited income. Mrs Charlton was always robbing Peter to pay Paul, because she just did not have enough money to pay for the necessities of life. That one penny per week to cover the cost of medical treatment was in fact beyond their means, but had to be found somehow, otherwise there would be no medical cover when it was needed. It was only through the strength and determination of Mrs Charlton that her daughter survived, others were not so lucky. They were also fortunate in receiving the services of the district nurse. Her help and support were invaluable. Her calming influence did so much towards gaining the confidence of her small patient and dissipating the mother's increasing anxiety.

The Provident Dispensary was situated in St. Michael's churchyard, as a means of providing a medical service to the poorest members of society for a fee of one penny per week. By 1888 it served approximately half the population of Coventry according to the *Victoria County History (Vol.VIII)*, with 20,000 members. In 1893 the Public Medical Services formed a rival organisation, restricting its members to those earning less than £2.00 per week. They considered the Provident too elitist, but took a rather moralistic tone by refusing to treat diseases associated with immorality or intemperance. They charged the same one penny fee as the Provident, but were not as popular, presumably because many potential patients were just those who suffered the effects of too much alcohol or venereal diseases.

From the diseases of childhood we move on to those that afflicted the young adult and how severely this could affect the family. Tuberculosis was not a disease of the poor, it could affect any age or class. There are two types, which infect man, the bovine and the human bacillus. The bovine type is spread through infected milk and meat and tends to be a disease of childhood. The human strain is spread by droplet infection. A considerable amount of research had been carried out in the nineteenth century to find the cause of the disease and discover an affective treatment or cure. Despite the fact that it was known that cattle carried the bacillus, which could be spread to humans, little was done to prevent it spread.

E. Hugh Snell, the Coventry MOH stated in his 1898 report that T.B. was a preventable disease. He was well aware that the disease was spread from animals to man via cows milk, as well as from improperly cooked meat. 60,000 people were dying of the disease every year in England and Wales. In Coventry the deaths from T.B. were consistently high.

Table 6.

1890=112	1894=105	1898=92
1891=92	1895=97	1899=113
1892=112	1896=105	1900=141
1893=100	1897=102	

Medical Officer of Health Report 1900

The first line of attack in eliminating the disease was the wide spread slaughter of herds affected. It was estimated that 30% of milk cows were infected. However, the farmers were unwilling to destroy their cattle without adequate compensation. The Corporation Act of 1900 was passed to try and stop the sale of tuberculous milk. A £10 fine could be imposed for allowing such milk to be sold. The onus was on the dairyman to comply, but he did not know whether the milk was infected or not, he had no way of testing the milk and pasteurisation was not universal at this time. In 1904 the T.B. (animals) Compensation Bill came up before parliament for the proposed payment of compensation for slaughtering animals with the disease and the destruction of the carcases. It failed after arguments about who should pay the cost. Not until 1922 did the government take steps to prevent the sale of unpasteurised or non-tuberculin tested milk.

For a family afflicted by the disease the consequences could be catastrophic. If it was the breadwinner, then the likelihood was a slow decline in family fortunes. The disease could take years to kill a person, but incapacity and weakness would prevent that person from doing a manual job as their strength declined. Beatrice Callow cites the case of Aunt Martha's son-in-law Ben, who was reduced to making cloth rugs to earn a little money as he slowly died of T.B. If it was the wife suffering from the disease, then the children could be neglected and might even end up in the workhouse. Most families must have known such cases where great poverty was caused by this disease.

Few people with the disease were isolated at this time, although there were those who advocated such measures. Most were left in their own homes to die slowly and painfully. There were differences of opinion on the benefits of fresh air and sunshine as a treatment, but for the poor this was not an option. There was no treatment, only recommendations for better management and prevention of the spread of the disease. The MOH recommended the disinfecting of utensils used by the sufferer, the use of a covered sputum pot, increased attention to cleanliness and washing, no kissing or hand contact and no dusting except with a moistened, disinfected cloth. After death the house would be thoroughly disinfected. In the 1903 MOH report there is a list of the occupations of the victims of T.B. that year, which illustrates that anyone was a possible victim.

23 cycle machinists, 18 housewives, 6 children, 6 watchmakers, 4 silkweavers, 3 carpenters, 3 labourers, 3 retired, 2 painters, 2 tailors, 2 dyers, 2 licensed victuallers, 2 domestics, 1 woodturner, tram conducter, coachbuilder, coalcarter, cab driver, groom, maltster, basketmaker, engine driver, bricklayer, school teacher and clerk.

Smallpox, once a terrifying disease, had been brought under control by the end of the nineteenth century following a national campaign of vaccination. However, a certain amount of complaisance had set in and children were not being routinely vaccinated to protect them. In 1888 an anti-vaccination movement was set up by people who objected to being forced into accepting vaccination and thought it a breach of their civil liberties. It required an exemption certificate from the court to register as a consciencious objector. In 1899 the MOH bewailed the fact that too many children were not being protected from the disease, but believed it was apathy, rather than consciencious objection, which was the root cause of the problem. There had been no cases of smallpox reported in the city for several years, although the disease was still taken very seriously by the authorities, for in 1899 a new isolation hospital at Pinley was opened.

In 1901 two cases of the disease were notified, the first for 5 years. Both male victims from London were isolated at Pinley and recovered. The public vaccinator was kept busy as people were galvinised into action to ensure they were protected. That year there was also a report of plague in Glasgow, when a man returned to Coventry after a stay in the hotel where the plague had been sited. He fortunately had no symptoms and the scare soon faded away.

An epidemic of smallpox hit Coventry in 1903 when 71 cases were reported to the MOH. Many of the victims were living in common lodging houses, where crowded living conditions could cause a rapid spread of the disease. Cases were immediately isolated; relatives and all contacts were urged to be vaccinated if they had not already done so. Many of the cases were mild to medium in severity, with only three deaths. In 1904 there were five cases notified, with 1 death and in 1905 just one case from a Much Park Street court.

The Workhouse
When people fell on hard times there was always the final recourse to the workhouse. This was a step that no one wanted to take, universally dreaded by the population. The workhouse was designed to be dreaded by the public, to reduce the cost of supporting the poor from the rates. It was thought that all provision for the poor could be contained within the workhouse, but it soon became evident that this was not possible. It was realised that it was often cheaper to give a charitable handout to support a family in their own home during a time of stress, than it was to take a whole family into the confines of the workhouse and find food, clothes and accommodation for them. During our period of research the figures show an increasing amount for outdoor relief and a fluctuating number of inmates.

Table 7.
Number of people receiving outdoor relief.
1897 = 376   1898 = 405   1899 = 502   1900 = 409   1901 = 578
1902 = 541   1903 = 809   1904 = 870   1905 = 820
Compiled from Medical Officer of Health Reports 1897-1905.

Table 8.
Expenditure of the workhouse.
1897 = £1,959 5s 7d
1898 = £2,072 6s 3d
1899 = £2,134 15s 8d
1900 = £2,683 12s 0d
1901 = £2,449 14s 3d
1902 = £2,458 2s 3 1/4d
1903 = £2,507 0s 8 3/4d
1904 = £2,857 13s 4 1/4d
1905 = £2,764 13s 7d
Compiled from Medical Officer of Health Reports 1897 - 1905.

Table 9.
Number of inmates at the end of the year.
1897 = 400   1898 = 452   1899 = 473   1900 = 406   1901 = 435
1902 = 429   1903 = 438   1904 = 491   1905 = 505
Compiled from Medical Officer of Health Reports 1897 - 1905.

When a family took the desperate step of resorting to the workhouse, the family was split up. Husbands and wives were separated, no matter how old, so it was not just to prevent them from having more children. Younger children stayed with their mothers, but once they reached the age of seven they too would be segregated. These children, deprived of love and care ended up like those in Beatrice Callow's school of St. Michael's, the nearest board school to the Whitefriars workhouse in Coventry. The school was obliged to take these children whether they liked it or not, and the impression was that they did not. Many of these children were illegitimate, abandoned by their mothers to the mercies of the workhouse system. No wonder Beatrice Callow thought they were sullen, uncouth and disagreeable. Their shaven heads marked them out from the other pupils, although probably used as a method of preventing head lice, which was so prevalent. She also complained that they wet themselves, but this was probably because they were too disturbed or scared of authority to ask to be relieved. Whatever the case their lives must have been miserable, without love or even kindness. As they reached school leaving age the boys could be apprenticed to a master without reference to the child and the girls were usually sent into service.

Women in the workhouse had to perform some kind of work to earn their keep. This involved cleaning, working in the kitchens or laundry. In the past they might have been allotted repetitive jobs like picking oakum, but that was rare by 1900. They might even work in the infirmary attached to the workhouse, cleaning or caring for the inmates. At a meeting of the Board of Guardians, reported in the *Coventry Herald* on the 17th February 1905, there was a move to detain women for one year within the confines of the workhouse, following the birth of an illegitimate child. There were women in the workhouse with 2, 3 or 4 illegitimate children; in fact they confirmed that there was a case every week received into the workhouse. This proposal was supported by the chairman and it was finally agreed that a woman producing more than one illegitimate child should be detained for three years. The motion was carried. This curtailing of freedom for these unfortunate women, who found themselves pregnant, was little less than imprisonment.

A high proportion of the inmates of the workhouse were elderly or infirm. When the old could no longer look after themselves, especially if they had no family, the only resort was the workhouse, an evil to be postponed as long as possible. Once taken to the workhouse infirmary, it was unlikely that a recovery would be made; death was the most common outcome. The final indignity was the ability of the medical profession to claim any pauper's body for research, or a pauper's grave. The Directory of 1893 includes the Board of Guardian's proceedings for that year. On 20th January it reported that there were 174 sick inmates. The infirmary was so full that fifty of them had to be accommodated elsewhere in the workhouse. The facilities of the hospital, built in 1889, were obviously inadequate at the time, with so many people going there to die. A new block was built at the workhouse in 1906 to fulfil the need. It was standard practice to use the mortuary at the workhouse for the city dead. The MOH complained constantly about the lack of a public mortuary, requiring bodies to be kept at home until burial, which might be a source of infection or nuisance.

Male and female inmates were expected to work a twelve-hour day in winter and thirteen hours in summer. Men were allotted tasks on maintenance of the building or using a trade that they had practiced outside the workhouse. Able-bodied men were encouraged to look for work as the institution was only intended as a stopgap while a man sought work. On 16th November 1893 the Board of Guardians reported that casual paupers, those just passing through, in the previous month had numbered 556. Of those, they considered only 115 were honestly in search of work. Once resident in the workhouse, rules were rigidly enforced. On 6th April 1905, the *Coventry Herald* reported the case of Frank Timms, aged 17, charged with absconding from the workhouse with his officially issued suit of clothes. He was soon arrested, for he must have been very distinctive and brought before the police court. He was found guilty and sentenced to 28 days in prison. Had he applied for release he would have been given a set of clothing. Perhaps it was an indication of the mind of a young person becoming institutionalised from long exposure to the life inside the workhouse. However, alternatively he may have considered prison a better option than the workhouse.

School

It was common practice for poor children to attend school from an early age to allow mothers either to go to work or look after other younger children. Living in crowded conditions, there was nowhere for children to play except the court or streets. The normal age to begin schooling was five, but if the school was willing they could attend as early as three years old. As Mrs Charlton found out when she sent Grace to school at three, there could be some censure from the neighbours who considered her too young.

St. Michael's School was situated in Much Park Street and therefore very convenient for the many children living in the numerous courts of the area. Built in the 1850s it accommodated around 700 children, boys, girls and infants. The 1874 Directory states that the average attendance was 150 boys, 130 girls and 140 infants. By 1900 the numbers had risen to 221 boys, 200 girls and 175 infants, a reflection of the greater enforcement of the Education Act of 1871. The older children's numbers were almost up to capacity, but the school could have taken nearly double the number of infants according to the 1900 Directory. At that time the Headmaster of the boys was Arthur Banks, the Headmistress of the girls was Miss Elizabeth Taylor and the infant's Headmistress was Miss Mary Agnes Long.

It is obvious that classes were large and discipline firm, to keep control of so many children. The offspring of some of the poorest members of society attended this school, including the workhouse children. Even the poorest children looked down on the pauper children. However, this was a relaxation of the original ethos of the Poor Law system, which required complete segregation of the children within the walls of the institution. By the end of the nineteenth century the authorities realised that the workhouse was not the best environment for children. Pauper children were being cared for in smaller units ouside the workhouse, where possible, and the attendance at a local school was part of that strategy.

Teaching concentrated on reading, writing and arithmetic, equipping youngsters with basic skills for the jobs they would do when they left school. The sewing class for girls described in *Hurdy Gurdy Days* was typical of instruction for girls to prepare them for domestic service or running a home of their own. At St. John's School the girls had to mend surplices for the church choir and darn numerous socks, while at Wheatley Street School, Selina Dix was pioneering domestic science and running lessons in household management for older girls.

The Church

Christ Church only acquired an independent parish in 1900. Before that it had been part of St. Michael's. It was a poor parish encompassing a network of courts and crowded streets including Much Park Street, but it also attracted a substantial number of important citizens and better-off artisans. There was a strong evangelical bias at Christ Church, firstly with the Rev. W. Kipling Cox from 1885 to 1894 and continued by the Rev. F.M. Brodie from 1897 to 1916. The aim of the church was to promote a Christian way of life, through hard work, thought for others, good works for those in need of help and a strong Temperance streak.

The Mission Room in Greyfriars Lane performed the function of a church hall in modern times. As Beatrice Callow relates it was used as a meeting place for the mothers of the parish to get together and relax from the cares of the home, while their young children were cared for in safety. Undoubtedly the Church was hoping to encourage the children to attend Sunday school and eventually become 'worthy' members of the community. The first meeting of the Juvenile Temperance Society was held in the Mission Room on 4th November 1890. Children were encouraged to sign the pledge without fully understanding the implications and many fell by the wayside in adult life.

The Mission Room was a multifunctional building, used throughout the week for meetings and entertainments. There was a Young Women's class, for the purpose of repairing old clothes to sell on, a Men's Bible class, Church Temperance meetings held fortnightly and a Children's Missionary sewing party, also Sunday school, Mission services and prayer meetings. Sales of work were held there, lectures and magic lantern shows were performed in the evenings. It was a very important focal point for the poorer members of the parish who might have felt in awe of attending services at the church.

An annual outing was organised by members of the committee for the children of the parish. Several times the children were taken to such venues as Stoneleigh Abbey, Quinton Pool and Brandon. The cost of transport was sometimes prohibitive, but they always managed to make the day enjoyable. If the parents could not afford the nominal fee, then the cost would come out of funds collected for the purpose. Between forty and fifty could not pay in 1903, however, the free tickets were not distributed until the evening before the event. The teachers too had their annual outing as a treat for all the hard work they invested over the year, although they had to bear the cost themselves. The expenses of the Mission Room and all the activities provided had to be collected from the better-off members of the congregation. Leading public figures such as John Gulson, the Iliffe family and numerous others made generous donations to the church and the Mission Room. Sometimes there was a deficit in Mission Room funds, which had to be made up from church funds and donations made a significant difference, for example in 1891 the rent of the Mission Room was paid by Mr H. Whiteman, a churchwarden.

Altogether the church did everything in its power to occupy the leisure time of its parishioners. To keep children off the streets, to give women a little time to themselves and to give men a purpose other than that of finding the nearest public house, was their object. The church organised a men's club, open every evening except Sundays and Wednesdays and by 1905 it was proposed that a gymnasium should be started to channel their energies into physical activities. The clergy went to great lengths to encourage working men to attend services, even to the point of disguising themselves and going into public houses to engage the attention of these men. It was probably only a minority who took up the challenge, like Beatrice Callow's father and his friends, but the clergy must have felt it to be worthwhile or they would not have done it.

Women made up a substantial number of the helpers in the church. Under-utilised women from middle class backgrounds found an acceptable outlet for their energy in good works. They made up a significant number of the committee members and the majority of the Sunday school staff. Rotas were compiled to make sure that there was enough staff to control the children when they attended church services, and as Beatrice Callow's father observed they could be very unruly, these teachers mostly consisted of women. When it came to organising outings it was the women who volunteered to cut up and distribute the food for their alfresco meals, look after the girls and younger children, while the men organised sports for the boys. When the Coronation procession was organised in 1902, it was the women who were expected to sew banners and order rosettes and sashes for the children. Without the support of the women of the parish the Church could not have achieved so much.

Conclusion

Hurdy Gurdy Days portrays a life of poverty in a congested inner-city area, but it is not a story of misery. Poverty to Beatrice Callow meant poor housing, second-hand clothes, the indignity of having to resort to the pawnshop on a regular basis and the contempt of professionals, like the doctor. However, there is never a suggestion that they went short of food or that the children were neglected in any way.

There were frequent moments of pleasure recalled by Beatrice Callow. The trips into town on a Saturday evening with her father, when a few pence provided her sister and herself with enormous enjoyment, whether in the form of an item of food or a toy. Pleasures were simple and cheap, but made all the difference to a life of hardship. The hurdy gurdy of the title was something the children could listen to, without the presence of parents. They could follow its progress, while the antics of the monkey entertained them as much as the music. All this for nothing, if there were no money to spare, but even the tiniest contribution would be gratefully received.

It was the mother who had the most arduous task of keeping the family fed, clothed and housed as decently as she could afford to. She is presented as a woman of intelligence, held down by her circumstances. Her wish to see her daughters well educated is probably why she sent them to school at the age of three. Education was a route out of poverty if used to advantage and maybe she regretted not having had the opportunity herself. She did not neglect their practical education either. She certainly had the drive and ambition in the family and took her husband and children with her.

Despite all their difficulties the family were not downtrodden. They had their pride, which remained intact regardless of setbacks and took them from the undesirable confines of a slum like Much Park Street to the clean, newly-built terraced home that they rented afterwards. It is significant that the progress of the twentieth century gave ordinary working class people the chance to fulfil their aspirations in a way that the nineteenth century did not.

Sources

City and Housing
Medical Officer of Health Annual Reports 1897-1905, E. Hugh Snell. Coventry Records Office CCHE/1/1/2&3.
Town Planning Report of 26th February 1912, J.E. Swindlehurst, City Engineer & Surveyor. Coventry Records Office.
Six Hundred Years of Municipal Coventry, Frederick Smith.
A Social History of Housing 1815-1985, 2nd Edition, John Burnett.
Twentieth Century Coventry, Dr. Kenneth Richardson.

Common Lodging Houses
Medical Officer of Health Annual Reports. op. cit.
Coventry Herald.

Drunkenness
Coventry Herald.
Medical Officer of Health Annual Reports. op. cit.

Neighbours
Workhouse death records. Local Studies, Coventry Central Library.

Health
Medical Officer of Health Annual Reports. op. cit.
Directories. Local Studies.
Victoria County History, Vol. VIII.
A Social History of Medicine, F. F. Cartwright.
Victorian and Edwardian Shop Workers, Wilfred B. Whitaker.

The Workhouse
History of Whitefriars.
Workhouse Children, Frank Crompton.
Victoria County History, Vol VIII.
Coventry Herald.

School
Directories.
Victorian Schools and Scholars, J.W.Dorling. Local Studies.
Growing Up Poor, Anna Davin.
Workhouse Children, Frank Crompton.

The Church
The Third Spire, Rev. Alan Munden.
Parish Magazines, Warwick Records Office. DR 1155/4/1-3
Minutes of Sunday School. Warwick Records Office. DR 1042/1

Epilogue

When I began my research into the conditions of the poor in Coventry at the commencement of the new century, I was determined to trace Beatrice Callow and her family. The final words of *Hurdy Gurdy Days* are '...but that is another story.' That story was the one I wanted to find and eventually I did. My first step was to look at the census records for 1891. This should have given me the number in Much Park Street where the Charltons lived. However, I was frustrated by finding no Charltons in the street at all. I looked at the Directories next, to see if there was any mention of the name Charlton. Here too I drew a blank, as the few Charltons I encountered were obviously not the ones I was looking for. As a very poor family, I thought it unlikely that Beatrice's father would have a vote, so there was little point in searching voters' lists.

I decided that as the Charltons could not be found, I would have to start from the other end, find Beatrice and work backwards. I put a notice in the *Coventry Evening Telegraph* appealing for information about Beatrice Callow. Only one reply came, suggesting a lead I might follow up, but it proved to be unconnected with my quest. I began searching the electoral rolls hoping for a clue, but as they are listed by street rather than by name, I found it a fruitless exercise. I perused telephone directories for the post war period and cross-checked all Callows with the electoral roll. Again I looked at the Directories, this time for Callows, but without success. I trawled through the St. Catherine's House death records from 1966-97 to find Beatrice's death, but although I found many Beatrice Callows, I could not find one who was registered in Coventry.

By this time I was beginning to despair of ever finding her and I even began to doubt the genuineness of *Hurdy Gurdy Days* and yet I knew instinctively that it was true. I eventually came to the conclusion that she had changed the names of her family and others featured in the story. That became obvious when I could not find a single person mentioned despite all my research. I decided to have another try at finding Beatrice by writing to every Callow in the Coventry and district telephone directory. The response was excellent. Within a few days I received many telephone calls from members of the Callow family. Most were extremely interested in the project I was working on and tried to help in every way possible. I even thought I had found her at last when Dr Callow informed me that both his mother and his sister were called Beatrice, but the dates and details of their lives did not tie up and I was back where I started.

The breakthrough came when a friend, Cathy Hunt, rang me one day in July 2000, some nine months after my search began, to say that she had found Beatrice Callow. While looking up some correspondence of Dr. Kenneth Richardson in Coventry Records Office, she had come across a reference to *Hurdy Gurdy Days*. Her suspicions were confirmed when she read the letters, copied down the address and noted the access number. Armed with these facts, the following day I was able to read the correspondence myself, hardly able to contain my excitement. I discovered that in 1971 when the exchange of letters took place, she was living in the little hamlet of Haselbury Plucknett, near Crewkerne, Somerset. She signed herself Beatrice M. Callow and that was another clue to her origins.

Once I was armed with this new information I was able to return to the St. Catherine's House records and find her death. Even then I found two possible references in the name of Beatrice M. Callow, a Beatrice Margaret Callow, born 15th August 1901, registered at Taunton in the March quarter of 1972 and a Beatrice May Callow, born 14th November 1898 registered at Chard in the March quarter of 1973. Both were possibilities as either registry office was within easy travelling distance of her home. I obtained both death certificates and found that it was Beatrice May Callow whom I had been pursuing for so long. This provided me with the information that her maiden name had been Raby and her husband's name was Hubert Arthur Callow. I then applied for her birth certificate, which gave me the address in Much Park Street and names of her parents. The following history of her family life I have gleaned from the records up to 1939, after that point all information was supplied by her elder son Philip Callow, an author himself, and her nephew David Callow, who rang me quite unexpectedly in September 2000, and put me in touch with his cousin Philip.

Much Park Street was a highly congested part of Coventry long before Beatrice was born in 1898. Her grandparents, Edwin James and Emma Raby lived in 13house 33court with their young son, also Edwin James, when the census was taken in 1881. Edwin James snr. aged 30 and described as a weaver, his wife Emma aged 29, was a cotton filler in a factory, while their son at 4 years old, was a scholar. By 1891 when the next census was taken the family circumstances had changed. Emma Raby was by then a widow, her husband having died the previous year at the age of 39. Her address had changed to 7house 33court Much Park Street and her occupation was described as charwoman. In the same house resided her son Edwin James then 14 whose occupation was listed as a rauphmaker, her daughter Florence Beatrice aged 3 and a female visitor Rohe or Roke Ward aged 12 and described as a scholar. Florence Beatrice died in 1896 aged 8.

Edwin James Raby Jnr. and Fanny Elizabeth Charlton were married early in 1898 and Beatrice May was born in November of that year. They had another daughter Florence Elizabeth born in 1901. The first entry for Edward (Edwin) James Raby at the Much Park Street address appears in the Voter's list for 1900. Beatrice movingly portrays family life in the house until 1905, when the determination of her mother Fanny, took them to a newly built terraced house at 32 Vecqueray Street. Emma Raby, Beatrice's grandmother, died in 1909 and her age is recorded as 56, which is not compatible with the census of 1881 or 1891.

Beatrice married Hubert Arthur Callow in 1923 and they moved to Birmingham where Philip was born in 1924. Florence married Ernest F.B. Jones, better known as Fred, in 1926. The Callow's moved into 30 Vecqueray Street, next door to Beatrice's father in 1928 and a second son, John, was born. Beatrice's mother Fanny died in 1928, at the age of 51, a factor which possibly influenced the move back to Coventry. They first appear on the electoral roll in 1929 at this address. By 1932 they had moved in with Beatrice's father, next door at number 32. As they were only two bedroomed houses the two boys had to share a bedroom with their grandfather, just as Beatrice and her sister had with their grandmother. Edwin James Raby died, aged 62, in the early part of 1940, as a result of being knocked over by a vehicle, Philip Callow believes in Trinity Street, during the blackout. As he was profoundly deaf he would have been unaware of an approaching vehicle in the poor visibility.

Hubert Callow became an A.R.P. warden in the war. During one of the heavy air raids that preceded the blitz, he was standing on the corner of Vecqueray Street when a landmine came down nearby. The blast from the impact sent the school wall, by which he stood, tumbling down on top of him. He sustained serious injuries to the face, including a badly broken jaw. He spent the next nine months in Bromsgrove hospital recovering.

The family was evacuated to Leamington where Aunt Florrie, who lived in the town, found them a basement flat. This turned out to be very basic, but they managed to make it comfortable. Hubert worked for an engineering company in Leamington for the rest of the war. The family returned to Coventry after the war and lived in Bassett Road, Coundon, near to Hubert's brother William. Hubert worked for Rootes at this time, but longed to get away from the grind of working as a clerk in a factory. Beatrice too had a dream of escaping city life and owning a cottage in the country with roses round the door.

Around 1947-8 they decided to go looking for their idyll in Somerset. They settled on 'Little Thatch' in the village of Haselbury Plucknett, a house in need of care and attention. The house was to be auctioned, a practice totally alien to them, but they plucked up their courage and went along. They had a very limited budget, but they succeeded in their quest, paying £700 for the small thatched cottage. Over the following years they modernised and repaired the house to suit their requirements.

At first Hubert became an insurance agent, out in the fresh air and free from the factory environment, but unfortunately it was not very lucrative. He was forced to take a job at Westlands in Yeovil, where he remained until his retirement at the age of 68. During the last few years of the 1960s Beatrice wrote *Hurdy Gurdy Days*, determined to record her experiences in childhood. Hubert, enjoying his retirement at last, was somewhat put out to find his wife retreating upstairs to write her memoir. He too decided to put pen to paper and write his own memoir, but as his son Philip remarked, it did not have the spark of emotion that his mother's writing possessed.

When finished, she tried to interest publishers in her manuscript, but each time it was dispatched, it would return a little more dog-eared than the last time. She remained optimistic, but Hubert often felt dispirited on her behalf. After Hubert's death in 1970 Beatrice carried on trying to excite some interest in her manuscript, but to no avail. In 1971 she made contact with Dr. Kenneth Richardson at Coventry University (Lanchester Polytechnic as it was known then), when she was visiting her sister-in-law Ivy, widow of Alderman William Callow. Perhaps Ivy Callow suggested the approach, knowing of Dr. Richardson's interest in the history of Coventry, through his interview with her husband. Beatrice handed her manuscript over to Dr. Richardson's assistant, Elizabeth Harris, at his office during August 1971. In her first letter to him, dated 30th August 1971, she remarks that she is sure that it would sell like hot cakes, if only it became available to the public.

In his reply of 8th September 1971 he was unable to give Beatrice any hope that it could be published in pamphlet form, but stated that they were establishing a tape library and that it might be useful to put it on tape for research purposes if she agreed. She replied in the affirmative on 12th September. Dr. Richardson wrote back on 7th October mentioning that the BBC intended to make a documentary about Coventry towards the end of February 1972 and that they might use short portions of the tape of *Hurdy Gurdy Days*. The reply from Beatrice came on 13th October to say that she thought it a good idea for parts to be used by the BBC, but that as the manuscript had been returned to her, she would have to send it back. On the 18th October the manuscript was returned to Dr. Richardson. In the accompanying letter she says, 'I have taken the precaution of registering it, as the writing entailed so much work, I didn't want to risk losing it.' He acknowledged receipt of the package on 21st October and returned the manuscript to her on 14th December 1971, thanking her and confirming that it would be a valuable addition to the tape bank.

Beatrice lived only a year after the correspondence ceased, she died on 31st December 1972, probably disappointed not to have seen her manuscript in print. It has taken almost thirty years to come to the notice of the public and be appreciated for its worth, as a valuable piece of social history.

Mother

When all she wanted was to be with him.
Idle at last, not knowing
how near she was, fearful above all
of how burdensome she must be.
Crying out repeatedly
to be forgiven –
"I'm such a nuisance!" –
with her servant's dread
of being waited on

and her lost front door,
helpless as a child at last,
shrinking with shame between the sheets.

Hospital tea came round
and she sat humbly,
thank you, thank you,
whispering in my ear afterwards
"It's terrible!"
A huge worry was the chicken,
bought for my homecoming that Christmas.
"I'll have to tell you what to do."

The phone told the rest.
How she had died. A time to come
for her belongings.
The voice stopped and I sat on,
as if I would never move.
As if the world had emptied.
As if the blow, immense, silent,
kept on descending.

Philip Callow, from *Nightshade and Morning Glory*, published 1998.

Family Tree

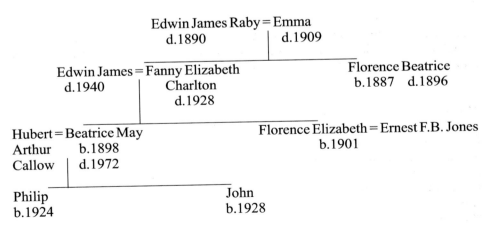

71

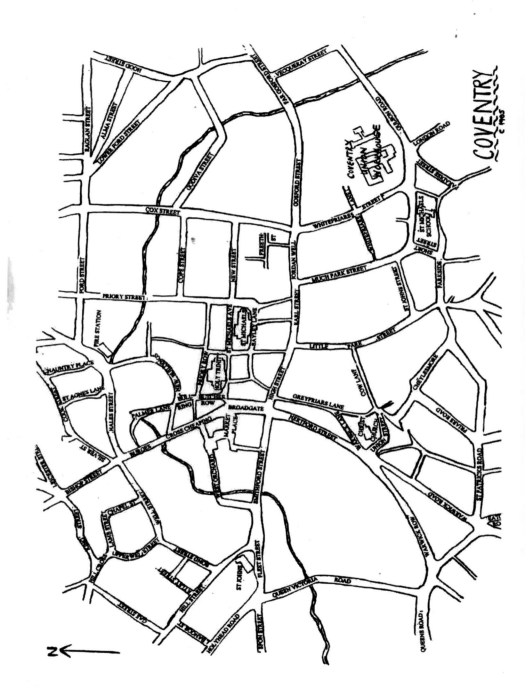

COVENTRY
c 1965